The Newlyweds' Guide to Investing & Personal Finance

by

Carrie Coghill Martin, CFP
with Evan Pattak

CAREER
PRESS

Franklin Lakes, NJ

The Newlyweds' Guide to Investing & Personal Finance
Edited by Dianna Walsh
Typeset by John J. O'Sullivan
Cover design by Foster & Foster Inc.
Printed in the U.S.A. by Book-mart Press

To order this title, please call toll-free 1-800-CAREER-1 (NJ and Canada: 201-848-0310) to order using VISA or MasterCard, or for further information on books from Career Press.

The Career Press, Inc., 3 Tice Road, PO Box 687,
Franklin Lakes, NJ 07417
www.careerpress.com

Library of Congress Cataloging-in-Publication Data

Coghill Martin, Carrie, 1965-
    The newlyweds' guide to investing & personal finance / Carrie Coghill Martin with Evan Pattak.
        p. cm.
    Includes index.
    ISBN 1-56414-573-5 (pbk.)
      1. Married people—Finance, Personal. I. Pattak, Evan M. II. Title
HG179 .M34255 2002
332.024'0655—dc21   2001054391

Acknowledgments

Writing is a collaborative art, and this book is no exception. It's true that only a few people were involved in the research and writing, but many more were instrumental in the education, support, and inspiration that made this work possible.

Among them are my clients at D.B. Root & Company, a group with rich and varied insights into the many components of financial security. Time and again, they've amazed me with the depth of their commitment to me and our company. Time and again, I've grown from my association with them.

I'd also like to thank David B. Root, Jr., my mentor and friend, for leading me on an unending journey of discovery. David's ability to teach and inspire is a gift; I'm just one of many grateful beneficiaries.

This book couldn't have been produced without the efforts of my writing partner, Evan Pattak, who found readable ways to express complex concepts and prodded me to transform bits of information into comprehensive, useful presentations.

"Each time I read one of our chapters, I realize I'm doing my own finances all wrong," Evan would say. But then, in his seeming despair, he would ask a penetrating question that would send me back to my files for more research.

Words can't express our gratitude to the late Patti Burns, the mutual friend who introduced me and Evan, and our profound sorrow at her untimely death in October 2001. Her loss has left a void for us; for her husband and our friend, Chuck Cohen; and for all of western Pennsylvania, which revered her as its favorite news anchor. Patti would have been pleased, in her selfless way, to see this work in print, and she would have dismissed any notion that she played a role in its creation. But she did, and we miss her.

Finally, I would like to thank my daughter. Kelli didn't write any of this book, although she did relinquish the computer long enough to allow Mom to get in a paragraph here and there. But it's the lessons that I've learned from and with Kelli that are at the heart of this guide.

What are those lessons? That financial harmony is important only because it leads to personal and familial harmony. That communication, trust, and caring are key elements in building a comfortable financial future. "It's the economy, stupid," has become a Beltway buzzword to remind us of the primacy of financial issues. I *know* about the economy. It's the people, stupid. That's what Kelli has taught me.

Contents

Introduction

Happy Families Are All Alike: They Have Their Finances in Order

In the traditional version of the American Dream, young men and women followed a sure path to familial and financial stability. They married early, often right out of high school. They knew that the husband would be the sole breadwinner, and the wife would rule over the domicile. Perhaps most importantly, money management was an uncomplicated matter, involving little more than passbook accounts and savings bonds.

Today, both romance and finance are a bit more complicated. Couples tend to marry later in life, meaning that each individual may bring to the union a variety of assets and needs that would have been unprecedented in those earlier, more predictable times. That implies the need for serious and detailed discussions about blending—or separating—assets.

Just as couples may have amassed financial assets well before marriage, they may have acquired obligations as well. Mortgages, credit-card debt, alimony, child support—all of these and more may be part of the marital package.

Single-breadwinner families, of course, have gone the way of the hula hoop and poodle skirts. Today, most couples require two incomes to afford the lifestyles they desire. Even if some spouses don't need to work, many elect to, for personal goals and self-fulfillment. Should those dual incomes be merged in a common household pool? Should they be kept distinct? Is some combination of both approaches the best? Clearly, these are questions that 21st-century just-marrieds must explore.

Finally, even as marriage is more complex today, the act of saving money for the future has become both art and science. Modern newlyweds may choose from a dizzying variety of investment and savings vehicles—everything from CDs to stocks to insurance policies to tax planning—that their parents and grandparents may never have considered. It's a rich variety, to be sure, but it's also a bewildering series of choices that many newlyweds defer...until it's too late to maximize their gains.

Against this background, our goal is to provide a readable guide to help couples understand the financial challenges they will face and the options available to help them successfully meet those challenges. This book addresses often complex issues with a commonsense approach that should help couples reach the best decisions for them. If it's true, as Tolstoy wrote, that happy families are all alike, it's probably because they have their financial houses in order.

Our guide begins with some of the most fundamental—and immediate—choices that confront newlyweds, such as determining who will pay which bills, who will take charge of which checking accounts and credit cards, how to purchase the homes and cars that are right for your circumstances, and acquiring all the insurance coverage you need without overdoing it.

Your financial objectives, of course, extend beyond these basics, and so does our guide. We'll explore the various planning strategies for such long-term goals as children's education and your retirement, and we'll provide a detailed look at the investment options that can get you there.

Finally, because we know that much of the advice we've gathered here may seem at first blush, excessively theoretical, or perhaps unrelated to anything you've experienced so far, we've included profiles of five couples who will tell you exactly how they handled all the financial questions of their marriages.

You'll meet Audrey Korotkin and Don Clippinger, who have successfully blended two seemingly irreconcilable careers: rabbi and turf writer. You'll look in on Shirley and Stan Angrist, who decided that Stan would manage the family's portfolio—but only if he could pass a performance test devised by Shirley. And you'll meet Sarah and Sam Miller, a couple who personify both the delights and financial vexations of marriage.

We're deeply grateful to our five couples for sharing parts of their lives with us and you. They're all real people with real stories...and the courage to tell them. Neither of us is quite sure we'd have displayed the same mettle had we been asked to let our financial hair down, but we're appreciative that our five couples did.

Apart from being lively and informative, our profiles serve to underscore what we believe are the two most important messages of this guide. Our first underlying principle is that financial game plans for newlyweds are like snowflakes: No two are alike. Couples have different needs and aspirations, a wide range of income levels, and varying assets and liabilities that they bring to the union. All these variables are factors in the financial blueprint you develop. Beware investment gurus who assure you they have found *the* way, which they will graciously reveal to you at their investment seminars, modestly priced at $50 per ticket. Here's cheaper, more reliable advice: There are many ways to financial security.

Our second theme is that the single most important step you can take to assure financial success as a couple is to communicate regularly with your partner. Begin with a firm understanding of your joint assets. Establish your monthly budget together. Develop your goals as a team, and modify them as a team. Teamwork is a common thread running through the stories of our five couples. Those who have come closest to achieving their goals are those who have brought the most teamwork to the process.

You might even go so far as to schedule a set time each week to review financial matters as a couple. We've closed each chapter with a section called "Pillow Talk" that provides some fun but practical exercises for your joint financial planning sessions. As newlyweds, you may have other things on your mind at bedtime, but among other virtues, the prospect of financial security can be a powerful aphrodisiac.

Chapter 1

The Checking Account Challenge: How Many...and Who's in Charge?

I t is our fervent hope that the romance in your marriage lasts forever, that your honeymoon continues long after the last droplet of Niagara Falls has dried on your brow, that your mutual love and affection endure longer than *Who Wants to Marry a Multi-Millionaire?* It is also our firm recommendation that you work out the right arrangements for household finances and payments, because any frustration generated here, over time, can sour your otherwise-healthy relationship and produce significant economic difficulties.

Think of it. You return from your honeymoon eager for all the joys of connubial bliss, and there in the mailbox, along with the belated wedding cards, are the realities of your new life together: bills. There's the mortgage or rent to pay. Electric power and heat. Phone and Internet service. Insurance payments and healthcare. Home phone, cell phone, fax phone.

Among the first questions that newlyweds must answer are these: Who will take responsibility for paying all this? Does all available money—including wedding gifts and income—go into a

single household pool? If it does, how is spending money for each spouse determined?

Most couples will find that paying routine and regular household expenses through checking is the easiest, most convenient way to go, although credit card payments and debits are an increasingly popular option. But who's in charge of the checkbook, and how should all household income be allocated? There are a number of potential approaches to the checking-account challenge.

I'm in charge here: the single checking-account approach

It was a staple of 1950s movies and television. There's Dad, surrounded by mountains of paper at his desk, running his hands through his hair and groaning, "Bills, bills, bills. How will we ever pay them all?" Mom wanders by with a perplexed look on her face, aching to be helpful but knowing that household finance is outside her domestic purview.

It may seem corny and dated in today's dual-income families where both wage earners enjoy a hearty measure of independence, but single checking-account families with one spouse in charge of all bill paying were the norm throughout most of America's history. For all its seeming obsolescence, the single-account approach has some advantages.

The most important benefit is the certainty it provides. One spouse pays all the bills and thus knows how much to budget for household expenses and has a firm sense of when each bill is due. Bill paying becomes a regular, predictable function; bills are likely to be paid on time and in full, without the annoyance and expense of late payment fees.

The second advantage of this approach is that it can play to the strengths of the couple. What we mean is that the skills associated with money management and bill paying are not necessarily divided equally. If one spouse excels at it and the other has little interest or aptitude in these matters, it may be logical to entrust a single checking account to one spouse only.

However, the downsides of the single-account system are equally obvious. Most importantly, the spouse without checkbook control may feel powerless, to say nothing of penniless. Nothing can prove more harmful to a marriage than a growing sense of dependence on the part of one spouse; in many cases, the single-account approach causes or deepens this divide.

In addition, if the spouse without checkbook control is contributing all income to the household pool, that spouse will be left without funds for ordinary living expenses. This raises the specter of the allowance, that is, a weekly or monthly sum provided to the partner without checkbook control. Many modern couples will recoil at the notion of an allowance, as it means dependence on the bill payer and suggests a subordinate role. It also implies regular negotiations about the size of the allowance. You can well imagine the scene: The spouse with the allowance forced to justify all expenditures under the harsh glare of "The Boss." For many, this is an unsavory prospect that introduces, even regularizes, conflict in a marriage and can lead to more serious problems in the relationship.

Among those problems: The spouse without checking-account control may be completely in the dark about finances, both generally and specifically. That may be fine if mutually acceptable, but what if the partner without control suddenly is *forced* to take control, due to divorce, illness, disability, or death? Welcome to Panic City. Perhaps most importantly, on a personal level, the suddenly-in-control spouse will be forced to learn about finances while under the emotional stress associated with one of these wrenching occurrences. You may not enjoy bill paying now; how much less will you enjoy it under these dramatic new circumstances?

For the single-account approach to work, couples must communicate frequently about the financial needs of the family, and neither partner must be judgmental about how the other partner's allowance is spent. If you and your partner share similar views about spending and saving, this method has a better chance to survive. But if one of you is a "saver," and the other is a "spender," you need to find common ground quickly.

Some couples adopt a modified version of the single-account approach: They maintain one account, but each partner can access it through an ATM card. We've seen this lead to conflict more often than not, when the partners don't tell each other about expenditures or forget to save ATM receipts. This may be the worst of all worlds. Neither spouse has comprehensive knowledge or control of the account, which is always a dangerous situation.

Still another related approach is the joint account, in which no check can be sent unless both parties sign it. On the surface, this would appear to equalize responsibility and contributions. And it can, if the couple discusses the payments before signing, so that each is aware of what is being spent. More commonly, the bill-paying spouse slaps a pile of checks in front of his or her partner and barks out, "Sign these." So much for mutual understanding.

Just as important, if you need your spouse's signature to cash a check, pay a bill, or deposit your paycheck, how independent are you really? Finally, what happens if bills must be paid now, and one of the spouses is out of town or otherwise unavailable to sign the checks? It can get messy, and many couples will want to consider a different approach.

Dividing responsibilities...and conquering the checking-account challenge

A more popular approach among today's couples is for each spouse to maintain a checking account, and for each to take on the responsibilities of paying certain bills. This can work well in the modern dual-income household, provided that each spouse is earning enough to cover all the assigned bills.

The advantages to this approach are several. First, neither of you is overwhelmed by the burden of paying every household bill and is unlikely to be found, as poor old stereotyped dad, slumped over the office table with piles of unpaid bills and worries. Second, you're sharing bill-paying responsibilities, and thus each of you feels like an important contributor to the financial foundation of your union. Finally, there are no agonized negotiations over allowances, as each of you is left with some resources that can be spent independently.

Independence may be the key word in a dual-account approach. This approach balances responsibility and independence, which to our way of thinking, should be a primary goal of all your financial arrangements.

Attractive as this method may seem, there are pitfalls. The first is that bills must be divided fairly. That is, each of you should be assigned bills commensurate with your income. This means regular reviews of bill assignments and possible adjustments to account for any changes in income.

This system also assumes that each spouse will be equally effective in paying bills on time. Let's face it, styles vary. If your style is habitual, and you regularly pay all bills on time, you may be rankled if your spouse is less dedicated to the task. In addition, if one partner isn't paying bills regularly, late charges will mount, and the couple's credit rating can be damaged.

One possible solution: Designate one spouse as the person responsible for the physical act of bill paying, while the other partner forwards his or her portion of household expenses to reimburse the bill payer. Some will find that effective; others will consider it needlessly complicated.

As with all matters of marital finances, it's important to know who's good at what activities, and the preferences and style of each partner. Communication remains the key to success, no matter the arrangement.

Three isn't necessarily a crowd

Yet another approach we've seen is to establish three checking accounts: one for household expenses and one for each of the two partners. In the most common version of this method, each spouse allocates a portion of income to a common household pool but keeps a portion in a separate checking account for independent expenses.

This approach preserves a measure of independence for each of you, but it also invites some of the problems of the single checkbook—specifically, all bill-paying responsibilities tend to fall on the shoulders of one spouse—and thus should be considered very carefully before implementation.

One decided advantage here over the dual-account approach: There is a common account, and it can be used to save money for big-ticket purchases and long-term goals. Without some mechanism for joint savings, it isn't clear who will pay to fix a leaky roof, or if either of you has enough money to cover the repairs. Trust us. If you don't have money saved in a joint account, the roof *will* spring a leak.

On-line is fine

A word about on-line banking: It works, and it can be a great boost for timesaving and efficiency.

If your bank offers on-line accounts, you can get started by setting up a list of creditors that accept on-line payments; many will, although you will encounter some exceptions. When you're ready to pay any bill, click on that creditor, type in the amount owed, and click your mouse again. That simply, your bill is paid.

You can make it simpler still by incorporating a recurring payment feature, so you won't have to enter each payment. Quite a few companies, utilities chief among them, can automatically deduct payment from your checking account. However, you may prefer the greater control afforded by on-line banking. You know exactly what you're paying, before it's deducted. With automatic drafts, the opposite is true. Only after the payment is taken do you learn the amount of the bill.

On-line banking also helps you keep on top of your account. Because you can go on-line and view up-to-date information as frequently as you like, it's easier to know where you stand. You can balance your checkbook on an ongoing basis, rather than waiting until month's end and sifting through 30 days' accumulation of paper.

That having been said, it's wise to remember that on-line banking isn't the be-all and end-all for your decisions about the number of accounts you should maintain. You and your spouse will need to work out the key issues—control, dependency, allowances—whether you're paying on-line or not.

Nevertheless, on-line payment can simplify all approaches to checking accounts. If you typically procrastinate in paying your bills, an on-line account will enable you to take care of those bills whenever you're at your computer. If you sometimes forget to record an ATM transaction, just go to your on-line account and it's there. If yours is a three-account family with all accounts at the same bank, you can transfer money into the joint account with the click of a button.

Who says technology can't help keep a marriage healthy?

Communication is key to financial success

Decisions about checking accounts should be among the earliest that newlyweds make. The bills won't wait for any protracted decision-making process on your part.

The key to successful arrangements here, as it is in most financial aspects of marriage, is regular communication. Get together early, even before the nuptials, and discuss the advantages of the single-, dual-, and three-account approaches. Develop a firm understanding of your own talents and preferences and those of your partner. Your discussions should include how much money each of you will need beyond household expenses and which system will help each partner contribute to the common good while maintaining a measure of independence. In each marriage, we find "I," "You," and "We." Your checkbook arrangements should work for each of those units.

Don't let fashion be your only guide. We know a couple who adopted the two-checkbook approach, dividing the bills between them. Income was not a problem, as the couple typically grossed about $130,000 per year. The husband, an unrepentant list-maker and, dare we say, anal-retentive type paid his assigned bills and balanced his checkbook each weekend. The wife, more fey than her partner, paid bills on those rare occasions when she could work up the enthusiasm for it, generating countless late payment fees and husbandly ire.

Early in their marriage, the wife recognized the problem and suggested they switch to a single checking account, that the husband pay all the bills, and that she be given an allowance. The husband, appalled by the notions of dependence and subservience that this approach implies, refused to change.

They've been at it this way for 26 years. With periodic angry outbursts, the husband thrusts a bill on his wife—this time the phone bill, next time the natural gas bill—and demands she assume responsibility for it, because she's not paying her share of the bills. The wife throws it on her pile and pays it whenever, producing yet another late payment charge and another quarrel.

This is a couple seduced by fashion, rather than one following the needs of its partners. With regular communication, you'll do better.

 *Pillow talk*

Here's a five-step approach to developing the right checking-account and bill-paying arrangements for your marriage.

Step 1—As a couple, discuss how much money each of you needs to maintain independence and to keep up with your personal expenses.

Step 2—Talk about your individual talents and skills. Is one of you more adept at math and account-keeping? Would one of you feel dependent if all bill paying were left to your partner?

Step 3—Based on Step 2, come to a preliminary understanding of how many checking accounts you need and whether they'll be individual or joint accounts. Maintain your flexibility, understanding that changing incomes and other conditions may require you to modify your approach.

Step 4—If you determine that you'll share bill-paying responsibilities, make a preliminary allocation of bills to each spouse. Remember that a 50-50 division won't work unless income is also divided 50-50. Instead, try to work out a system that maintains a proportional allocation: The percentage of the total amount to be paid by each of you is roughly equivalent to the percentage of total household income contributed by each of you. Here are some bills you'll need to assign, though the list will vary from couple to couple:

$ Rent/Mortgage.
$ Basic telephone.

- $ Long-distance telephone.
- $ Cell phones.
- $ Electric power.
- $ Natural gas.
- $ Water.
- $ Sewage.
- $ Automobile insurance.
- $ Automobile maintenance.
- $ Automobile fuel.
- $ Healthcare costs (insurance contributions, copayments, and other costs not covered by your plan or plans).
- $ Internet service.
- $ Appliance insurance (computers, refrigerators, washers, dryers, for example).
- $ Cable television.
- $ Taxes (when not handled through payroll deductions).

Step 5—Check with your spouse regularly, perhaps at the end of each month, to make sure the arrangements are working for each of you.

Chapter 2

Planning Your Household Budget and Managing Debt

Merely mention the word *budget* and you evoke images of Ebenezer Scrooge at his counting desk, pinching pennies for the sheer delight of it, refusing to authorize any expenditures lest they defile his precious columns. Thanks to Scrooge and other depictions of curmudgeonly bean counters, budgeting has an enduring bad rap that all financial planners—most particularly you, as you consider household spending—must overcome.

Most people still perceive a household budget as a financial straightjacket that takes all the fun out of life. The thought of having to account for the money they spend, or even be aware of where they spend it, is an intimidating, unsettling prospect for most. Even the most enthusiastic proponents of budgeting will acknowledge that budgets *are* restrictive and that they *do* limit how you spend and where you spend. And that doesn't feel particularly good.

When two people unite in marriage, the reluctance to budget can grow even deeper. After all, here are two

people with potentially different approaches to spending and saving. Developing a monthly blueprint that accommodates both philosophies can be a prospect so daunting that most couples don't even make the effort.

With this type of mind-set, it's easy to see why budgeting is feared, and why traditional marital spending plans typically fail. Even couples with the best of intentions tend to view their budgets in the same way they regard diets. The first time they overspend in any one category, they liken it to gorging on that fatal slice of triple chocolate delight, figure that they've blown it, and toss the whole budget out the window.

If this has been your approach, stop and consider how others use budgets. Every corporation in America uses a budget to guide its spending. Every nation, every state in the Union, similarly develops a spending plan. What do they know about budgeting that you may not have grasped?

Simply this: Budgeting may be a way of managing your spending, but that is not the end in itself. The goal of all budgeting is to enable those who follow the budget to meet their larger financial objectives. If it's true for corporations and countries, it's true for your marriage as well. When you plan and follow a budget, you're taking an important step towards your most cherished financial goals. Most people let their spending habits direct their goals; it's your goals and how you would like to live your life that should direct your spending habits. Your budget is merely a tool, albeit an important one, to help keep you on course.

Budgets are restrictive, but only superficially. In fact, budgeting can create independence and freedom. Our ability to mold our lives is much greater than it was in most periods of our history. Think of the traditional 20th-century family. Typically, the husband was the sole breadwinner, working for one company for 40 years before retiring with a modest pension. If there were health insurance and other benefits, those were dictated by the employer. To a large degree, family finances were employer-directed. Some employers were more generous than others, but all employer-directed plans tended to limit the flexibility of the families they were supposed to be aiding.

Today, the choices are richer and more complex. No longer does Corporate America take care of us; we take care of ourselves through our own financial planning. It's a heady environment, this new financial freedom of ours, but it's one in which we do need a game plan to guide us to our goals. That's what budgeting can do.

By the end of *A Christmas Carol,* Scrooge had it right. Oh, he still fussed with his columns, but he realized now that his fussiness had goals: to help him fund that contribution to the ladies' aid society, purchase the goose for Christmas dinner, and still have enough left over to finance Tiny Tim's surgery. (Of course, Tiny Tim didn't need approval from his primary-care physician, and Bob Cratchett didn't have to worry about whether his time off would be covered under the Family and Medical Leave Act, but we'll save that for another chapter.) In short, budgeting helped Scrooge realize his financial and personal goals.

It will help you do the same.

3 steps to successful budgeting

Step 1—As a couple, discuss and establish your goals.

You don't need a post-mortem visit from Jacob Marley to rattle your chains and get you off the budgeting mark. What you do need is plenty of conversation as a couple to determine your personal and financial goals. With financial flexibility as the key to long-term happiness in the 21st century, how do you and your spouse want to live? You may, for example, choose to pursue the traditional American Dream of a big house, fancy car, and country-club membership. But through the planning and budgeting process, you'll come to realize the trade-offs involved—and what you may not be able to achieve if you pursue your primary goals.

Before putting pencil to paper, explore the following questions with your spouse:

What kind of house will satisfy you?

Although the last several decades have brought financial turbulence, one constant remains: Your home likely will be the largest purchase you ever make. Thus, it goes without saying that you and your spouse should have detailed discussions about your housing plans.

There are options here. Some couples might prefer to spend less on a house and more on travel. Others plan to entertain frequently and likely will be spending most of their time at home. Or they may anticipate having relatives living with them, either permanently or for extended periods. Therefore, they want a spacious, well-appointed home.

These are vital issues for you to consider because they relate directly to your ability to reserve and allocate resources for your other lifetime goals. The bottom line on house selection is this: The more money you spend on your home, the less you'll have for other objectives.

How will you get around locally?

We're talking here about your transportation needs. How will you get from here to there? If the answer is by car, the transportation category could be the second most expensive in your budget.

Couples who live in major metropolitan areas with superior transit systems (such as New York City and Chicago) may be able to use public transportation to and from work, shopping, and recreation, renting cars only for those special travel occasions. This may be a less expensive option than purchasing and maintaining automobiles, but it's simply not available for many couples.

If public transportation isn't an option in your situation, will you need two cars, or can you get by with one? Remember: Being able to afford two cars isn't the same as *needing* two cars. As part of your discussions about transportation, you'll want to explore which part of your local travel needs can be met by public transportation, car pooling, and any transportation resources that your employer or employers may offer.

Are you planning a family?

Although you may not be ready to answer this question in detail (that is, how many children you want and when they might come along to be left for future marital discussions) it's still wise to factor in the concept of financial planning for a family. Your dreams of raising a family in the future can be a key determinant in how you structure your spending today.

For example, if your plans for the next few years include starting a family, you may want to abstain from such major purchases as an expensive home, knowing that you'll need a sizable portion of your budget for raising your children. Remember, too, that starting a family can affect your budget on the revenue side as well. During your child's first few years, is one of you likely to put your career on hold to stay at home? If that's the case, your income and the ability to undertake major purchases could be dramatically reduced. We'll cover financial planning for family needs in much greater detail in Chapter 11.

What are your favorite leisure activities?

Budgeting isn't about abstaining from the things you enjoy. It's about developing the wherewithal to do these things more often. Is your favorite leisure activity travel? Dining out? Volunteering with civic and nonprofit groups? Identifying the activities that you and your spouse enjoy will allow you to specify the costs involved with your preferred activities. Do this, and you can incorporate these costs into your budget.

There's an additional benefit here as well. If you and your spouse are doing the things you most enjoy, you're more likely to build the strong bonds that are the basis of every successful marriage.

When do you plan to retire, if at all?

This may seem an odd question, particularly for couples just beginning their careers, but how you answer it can have both immediate and long-term effects on your budget.

For the longest time, our society considered 65 the "normal" retirement age. This stemmed from a decision by the federal government in the 1930s to begin Social Security payments at that magic age. Since then, much has happened to turn the conventional wisdom about retirement on its ear.

For one thing, people are living longer. The average life expectancy back in the 1930s was 64; today, according to the National Center for Health Statistics, the average male lives to the age of 76.5, the average female to the age of 79.4. Perhaps more significantly, if a man reaches the age of 60 today, he can expect to live for nearly 16 more years. For a woman, that figure exceeds 19 years.

Our parents and grandparents didn't have to plan for a huge retirement nest egg; statistics told them they wouldn't be around for very long following their retirement. The same is hardly true today, when the typical couple might need enough money to support themselves for about 35 combined post-retirement years. Clearly, financing your Golden Years requires a fair amount of gold.

Many people today covet an earlier retirement. They expect to remain vigorous and curious for several post-retirement decades, and they'd like to travel and explore new possibilities. Financing that active retirement requires expert planning over a lengthy period.

Conversely, now that we're living longer and staying healthier in our later years, many people choose to keep working well past the age of 65. Some even use their Golden Years to explore new education and career options. This trend has been reinforced by the realization that older people make excellent employees. They're seasoned, they're reliable, and they can serve as mentors for younger staff. According to the U.S. Census Bureau, the American workforce in March 2001 included more than 4.45 million people 65 and older, representing 13.7 percent of all Americans in that age group. And, with more than 5.1 million workers between the ages of 60 and 64, the number of seniors at work is sure to swell.

A decision to keep working past the customary retirement age has implications for your budget. You won't need to allocate as much of your budget to savings, and you'll be able to count on additional income in your later years.

Thus, bizarre as it may seem, achieving your goals as a couple requires you to consider your retirement now. Not only will you develop some specific planning points, but you'll also refine your long-term objectives. As you work on those objectives, you'll be helping your partnership to grow.

•••

As you consider these five key questions about your goals as a couple, keep in mind that each decision involves trade-offs. A large house today means less money available to raise a family. Early retirement implies a greater emphasis on savings. It's vital for you and your spouse to establish a general consensus on financial goals, so that the inevitable trade-offs don't become sources of resentment as the years pass.

Step 2—Create the budget.

Once you've reached a working understanding of the goals of your marriage, it's time to start applying those to your monthly budget. On page 47 is a budget form that we find useful in our own lives; it's sufficiently general and all-encompassing to apply to most couples. Before we consider some examples of a monthly budget, let's review some of the assumptions.

First, successful budgeting begins with precise knowledge of your monthly income. This may seem painfully obvious, but our experience suggests that people often begin from incorrect income estimates. If, for example, you and your spouse each have a job with an annual salary of $36,000, you could get at your monthly income by taking the combined gross income of $72,000, dividing by the 12 months in the year, and arriving at budgetable monthly income of $6,000, right? Wrong. What you've arrived at is a gross figure that doesn't allow for payroll deductions.

Typically, your employer deducts federal, state, local, and Social Security taxes from your pay. Your contribution to health insurance is also deducted, as are any union or professional association dues. The net income after all these deductions can be dramatically less than the gross figure.

Actually, you have two choices here. You can begin with the gross salary figure and include a category for "Payroll Deductions" in your budget, or you can simply base your budget on the actual income you receive each month. Either approach will work. The key is making sure you begin with the right income figure.

On the expense side, we suggest breaking these down into "Family Expenses" and "Individual Expenses." This configuration will enable you to shape your budget to your joint goal decisions while permitting each of you the degree of independence you've decided you need. For example, if you're a "three checking-account family," with one account dedicated to household expenses, having categories for "Family Expenses" and "Individual Expenses" will dovetail nicely with the payment responsibilities that have been assigned.

Make your budget as detail-oriented as you would like. We believe that the more detail, the better, in terms of gaining an understanding of your spending habits. However, if details aren't your thing and will impede your budgeting process, try to consolidate categories into "Fixed Expenses," "Variable Expenses," "Necessities," and "Discretionary."

Other consolidated categories can work as well. For example, you and your partner may prefer to use cash for household items such as spot grocery purchases, fuel, and dry cleaning. Instead of having a separate category for each item, you can consolidate these into a "Cash for Household Items" category. Some couples simply find fewer categories less intimidating and easier to adhere to.

Finally, remember to incorporate a line item in your budget for "Unforeseen Expenses." It's with some reluctance that we recommend this, because some couples will misuse this as an elastic clause they stretch to accommodate any whimsical purchase. We've seen new cars and luxury travel styled as "Unforeseen Expenses." Usually, they're not "Unforeseen Expenses"; usually, they're "Undisciplined Expenses."

If you want a new car or a nice vacation, just plan for it rather than get yourself in a financial bind through big-ticket, spur-of-the-moment purchases. It *is* important to maintain cash reserves to cover six months' expenses in case of a dramatic event, such as job loss. However, if you plan properly, stick to your plan, and protect yourself with the proper insurance (see Chapter 3), your "Unforeseen Expenses" category won't run amok.

Now you're ready to pencil in your budget. Here are several examples of what your monthly budget might look like, each using the premise of a two-job couple with gross annual income of $72,000. We'll use that gross income as our base; that will require us to establish a category for "Payroll Deductions"—and make us more aware of the impact of those deductions. The first example is on the next page.

Sample Budget #1: The Starter

	Monthly Expenses	Monthly Totals	Annual Expenses	Annual Totals
Employment Income		$6,000		$72,000
Less:				
Payroll Deductions				
Federal Income Tax	$808		$9,696	
*State Income Tax	$168		$2,016	
Social Security Tax	$372		$4,464	
Medicare Tax	$87		$1,044	
Health Insurance	$50		$600	
401(k) Contributions (5%)	$300		$3,600	
Total Payroll Deductions		$1,785		$21,420
Joint Fixed Expenses				
Rent	$900		$10,800	
Renters' Insurance	$20		$240	
Household Supplies/Maintenance	$50		$600	
Food	$300		$3,600	
Utilities:				
Gas, Electric	$120		$1,440	
Phone	$40		$480	
Cable	$40		$480	
Internet Service	$20		$240	
Medical/Dental	$25		$300	
Life Insurance	$12		$144	
Total Joint Fixed Expenses		$1,527		$18,324
Joint Discretionary Expenses				
Dining Out	$183		$2,196	
Entertainment	$300		$3,600	
Vacations	$166		$1,992	
Unforeseen Expenses	$83		$996	
Contributions/Subscriptions/Dues	$30		$360	
Savings/Investment	$330		$3,960	
Total Joint Discretionary Expenses		$1,092		$13,104
Husband-Fixed Expenses				
Car	$350		$4,200	
Transportation Costs/Maintenance	$83		$996	
Car Insurance	$100		$1,200	
Cell Phone	$50		$600	
Wife-Fixed Expenses				
Car	$350		$4,200	
Transportation Costs/Maintenance	$83		$996	
Car Insurance	$100		$1,200	
Cell Phone	$50		$600	
Total Individual Fixed Expenses		$1,166		$13,992
Husband-Discretionary Expenses				
Clothing	$83		$996	
Personal Care Services/Products	$30		$360	
Hobbies/Gifts	$75		$900	
Unforeseen Personal Expenses	$25		$300	
Wife-Discretionary Expenses				
Clothing	$100		$1,200	
Personal Care Services/Products	$42		$504	
Hobbies/Gifts	$50		$600	
Unforeseen Personal Expenses	$25		$300	
Total Discretionary Expenses		$430		$5,160
TOTAL EXPENSES		$6,000		$72,000

*State Income Tax estimated at 2.8% - check your state

Although there is no "typical" budget, because there is no "typical" household situation, Sample Budget #1 is a good model for many to follow. We call it "The Starter" because it can work well for newlyweds who haven't yet purchased a home and still are renting. Without that big housing nut each month, this budget can include a car for each spouse, generous discretionary expenses, and substantial savings/investments of nearly $4,000 per year.

You will note several other points about The Starter and our other sample budgets. You'll notice that after payroll deductions, the spendable portion of the $72,000 in employment income is $50,576, about 70 percent of gross income. No matter your income level, it's wise to keep this 30 percent shrinkage in mind. Also, check out the three "Unforeseen Expenses" categories, including discretionary and individual unforeseen expenses. These total $1,600, only about 3 percent of expenditures after payroll deductions. This allocation should remain constant, no matter how your circumstances may change.

Think of Sample Budget #2 (on the next page) as "The Big House." It features the purchase of a large home, but you may feel like you're in "the big house" as you try to keep up with the costs of your residence. The annual rent of $10,800 that we saw in Sample Budget #1 has given way to $24,000 for mortgage payments, taxes and insurance. Expenses for home maintenance and utilities also have increased accordingly.

To compensate for greater housing expenses, this budget eliminates one car and one cell phone while slashing such discretionary items as entertainment, dining out, vacations, clothing, and hobbies. Perhaps most importantly, the emphasis on the residence forces a reduction in annual savings and investments, from nearly $4,000 to just more than $1,100 per year. That could have serious repercussions over time.

Sample Budget #3 on page 33 is "The Balanced Approach." It envisions purchase of a smaller home than Sample Budget

Sample Budget #2: The Big House

	Monthly Expenses	Monthly Totals	Annual Expenses	Annual Totals
Employment Income		$6,000		$72,000
Less:				
Payroll Deductions				
Federal Income Tax	$808		$9,696	
*State Income Tax	$168		$2,016	
Social Security Tax	$372		$4,464	
Medicare Tax	$87		$1,044	
Health Insurance	$50		$600	
401(k) Contributions (5%)	$300		$3,600	
Total Payroll Deductions		$1,785		$21,420
Joint Fixed Expenses				
Mortgage	$2,000		$24,000	
Household Supplies/Maintenance	$100		$1,200	
Food	$300		$3,600	
Utilities:				
Gas, Electric	$166		$1,992	
Phone	$40		$480	
Cable	$40		$480	
Internet Service	$20		$240	
Medical/Dental	$25		$300	
Life Insurance	$12		$144	
Total Joint Fixed Expenses		$2,703		$32,436
Joint Discretionary Expenses				
Dining Out	$83		$996	
Entertainment	$150		$1,800	
Vacations	$84		$1,008	
Unforeseen Expenses	$83		$996	
Contributions/Subscriptions/Dues	$30		$360	
Savings/Investment	$93		$1,116	
Total Joint Discretionary Expenses		$523		$6,276
Husband-Fixed Expenses				
Car	$350		$4,200	
Transportation Costs/Maintenance	$83		$996	
Car Insurance	$100		$1,200	
Wife-Fixed Expenses				
Transportation Costs/Maintenance	$50		$600	
Cell Phone	$50		$600	
Total Individual Fixed Expenses		$633		$7,596
Husband-Discretionary Expenses				
Clothing	$66		$792	
Personal Care Services/Products	$30		$360	
Hobbies/Gifts	$50		$600	
Unforeseen Personal Expenses	$25		$300	
Wife-Discretionary Expenses				
Clothing	$84		$1,008	
Personal Care Services/Products	$42		$504	
Hobbies/Gifts	$34		$408	
Unforeseen Personal Expenses	$25		$300	
Total Discretionary Expenses		$356		$4,272
TOTAL EXPENSES		$6,000		$72,000

*State Income Tax estimated at 2.8%-check your state

Sample Budget #3: The Balanced Approach

	Monthly Expenses	Monthly Totals	Annual Expenses	Annual Totals
Employment Income		$6,000		$72,000
Less:				
Payroll Deductions				
Federal Income Tax	$691		$8,292	
*State Income Tax	$168		$2,016	
Social Security Tax	$372		$4,464	
Medicare Tax	$87		$1,044	
Health Insurance	$50		$600	
401(k) Contributions (12%)	$720		$8,640	
Total Payroll Deductions		$2,088		$25,056
Joint Fixed Expenses				
Mortgage	$1,600		$19,200	
Household Supplies/Maintenance	$83		$996	
Food	$300		$3,600	
Utilities:				
Gas, Electric	$150		$1,800	
Phone	$40		$480	
Cable	$40		$480	
Internet Service	$20		$240	
Medical/Dental	$25		$300	
Life Insurance	$12		$144	
Total Joint Fixed Expenses		$2,270		$27,240
Joint Discretionary Expenses				
Dining Out	$83		$996	
Entertainment	$150		$1,800	
Vacations	$84		$1,008	
Unforeseen Expenses	$83		$996	
Contributions/Subscriptions/Dues	$30		$360	
Savings/Investment	$223		$2,676	
Total Joint Discretionary Expenses		$653		$7,836
Husband-Fixed Expenses				
Car	$350		$4,200	
Transportation Costs/Maintenance	$83		$996	
Car Insurance	$100		$1,200	
Wife-Fixed Expenses				
Transportation Costs/Maintenance	$50		$600	
Cell Phone	$50		$600	
Total Individual Fixed Expenses		$633		$7,596
Husband-Discretionary Expenses				
Clothing	$66		$792	
Personal Care Services/Products	$30		$360	
Hobbies/Gifts	$50		$600	
Unforeseen Personal Expenses	$25		$300	
Wife-Discretionary Expenses				
Clothing	$84		$1,008	
Personal Care Services/Products	$42		$504	
Hobbies/Gifts	$34		$408	
Unforeseen Personal Expenses	$25		$300	
Total Discretionary Expenses		$356		$4,272
TOTAL EXPENSES		$6,000		$72,000

*State Income Tax estimated at 2.8%-check your state

#2 calls for, reducing the cost for mortgage, taxes, and insurance from $24,000 to $19,200. But instead of reallocating that money to discretionary expenses, Sample Budget #3 features heavier emphasis on savings and investments, including Roth IRAs and greater contributions to 401(k) plans, which lowers federal income taxes.

These are but three examples of a limitless variety of budget options. Whatever the differences in those options, the common denominator is trade-offs. Most of us *can't* have it all—at least, not right away—so we must understand our goals, prioritize them, and plan accordingly. If you want that palace early in your marriage, you must appreciate and accept the attendant sacrifices in other categories. Conversely, if saving for early retirement is your key objective, then you must be prepared to live more modestly now. Remember, your goals should drive your spending, not the reverse.

Step 3—Monitor and modify your budget.

As each of our sample budgets shows, the goals you share with our spouse will shape your spending plan. But goals change over time. You may have no immediate interest in starting a family, for example, but that could change a year from now. If it does, your budget and its emphases must change along with your goals. Circumstances change as well. Your income levels will rise or fall, depending on new jobs, salary/benefits changes at current positions, and layoffs. Clearly, changes in budgetable income will affect your spending plan.

In our technological age, many reliable software programs are available to help you monitor your budget. In addition, online banking is an excellent tool for keeping up to date on your checking accounts. It provides data that can be downloaded quite easily into your budgeting software, generating easy-to-use reports to help guide your decisions.

Beyond the technology that can facilitate monitoring, keep in mind that budgeting is not static. It's a process that involves becoming aware of your goals and spending habits, as individuals and as a couple, and communicating what you learn with your spouse.

Inevitably, the time will come when one of you blows a portion of the budget. Don't view it as a catastrophe, or a pretext for recriminations or scrapping the entire budgeting concept. Rather, let it be a catalyst for a calm review of your goals and spending habits that may lead to modification of your budget. As with most of the financial aspects of marriage, regular communication is the key to success.

Staying out of significant debt doesn't hurt either. In fact, the subjects of debt avoidance and debt management are so vital to successful budgeting that they merit a separate discussion.

Avoiding the debt net

Whoever called death and taxes life's only certainties clearly never used a credit card or purchased a home or car. To finance our modern lives, debt is as inevitable as those other two verities. Yet uncontrolled debt is a homewrecker, the torpedo that can roil tranquil waters and sink your marriage. Lest you think that we're getting carried away with the metaphor, consider these statistics.

According to the American Bankruptcy Institute, in the year 1980, there were 287,570 consumer bankruptcy filings in America; in that year, debt payment as a percentage of overall consumer spending was about 12 percent. Now, flash forward to the year 2000, which saw 1,217,972 consumer bankruptcy filings, an increase of more than 323 percent from the 1980 figure. In 2000, debt payment as a percentage of overall consumer spending was about 13.5 percent. It would take a more sophisticated study than this to determine the precise impact of consumer debt on personal bankruptcy, but it seems clear that the relationship is strong and frightening.

If those figures don't scare you into fiscal responsibility, ponder this one as well. In 2000, 97.17 percent of all bankruptcy filings in America were for consumer bankruptcies.

Part of the problem is that debt is a hydra-headed monster. It takes the form of mortgage payments, auto financing, credit-card interest, and interest on loans for home improvements and other activities. Very few of us ever take the time to add up our obligations in these various categories of debt; if we did, the total might shock us back to a cash-only approach.

Managing debt effectively

When we finally decide to rein in our debt, many of us get aggressive, determined to storm the debt beach in a D-Day-type offensive. We take every dime of our excess cash flow and apply it to our debt load. The problem with this "all or nothing" approach is that when an unexpected cost comes along, you're left with no alternative but to increase your debt to pay for the surprise expense. The debt cycle can begin all over again.

Instead of going hell-bent for leather, slow down and apply these two principles:

$ Get out of debt quickly and efficiently.
$ Incur as little future debt as possible.

Stating the principles is easy; implementing them can be tough. We're familiar with many debt-management scenarios. Some couples pay off their smallest debts first; if nothing else, they get a feeling of accomplishment that reinforces their debt-management initiative. Others shift their debt from credit card to credit card, exploiting attractive introductory rates on balance transfers. This works well enough, provided you're able to pay off the principal before the introductory period ends and the higher APR kicks in.

However compelling these schemes seem, there is no quick fix to debt management. Instead, consider these four steps to efficient debt management, always keeping the underlying principles in mind.

Step 1—Reduce your interest rates.

Pursue several strategies here. First, prioritize your debt with the highest interest charges. Let's say you're carrying an auto loan at 10 percent interest and credit-card debt at 20-percent interest. Your objective here should be to retire the credit-card debt first, because its interest rate is punishing. Once you've prioritized certain debts, pay the minimum on everything else.

Another strategy is to negotiate lower interest rates with your credit-card companies. The field has become so competitive that some credit-card issuers are offering year-round rates of 9 percent to 11 percent, compared to the 18 percent to 21 percent that had been standard. If the issuers of your credit cards are unresponsive and won't lower their interest rates, shop around for better rates and don't hesitate to switch cards. You can transfer all or part of your current debt to your new cards at lower interest and your savings will continue on new purchases.

This implies that you're paying attention to the interest rates you're paying. If you're not, now is the time to start.

Finally, consider consolidating your debt through lower-interest vehicles. Let's take a look two of the most popular.

Debt-consolidation loans

Here's the way these loans work. A lender, most typically a bank, lends you enough money to pay off all your debt. The interest rate charged by the bank can be substantially lower than that for the debt you just retired, resulting in potentially significant savings.

Debt-consolidation loans help in another way. In many cases your payment to the bank is a fixed amount, rather than discretionary. That promotes discipline.

Several cautionary notes on debt consolidation. Beware of banks or other lenders that promote consolidation without offering you a lower interest rate. There's little value to debt consolidation if your interest rates aren't reduced.

Also, once you've used your consolidation loan to pay off your credit-card debt, the best thing to do with your credit cards is destroy them—particularly those that charge exorbitant interest rates. Cut them up, have a plastic parade, do anything you want with them—except preserve them. If you hang onto them "for a rainy day," the temptation to incur new debt with credit-card purchases may prove irresistible.

Home-equity loans

These are among the most attractive of debt vehicles because the interest rate—sometimes 10 percent or lower—is more reasonable than that for most credit cards. In addition, the interest charges on home equity loans may be deductible for tax purposes, depending on your personal situation.

The catch, of course, is that your house becomes collateral for the loan; if you default, you can be forced to sell your home to satisfy the debt. In that situation, most loan agreements specify that the loan be paid off before you receive any proceeds that may remain. Thus, if you default here, you could be without your domicile and without any immediate cash to show for it. That's known as a bad day. Think twice about a home-equity loan if you envision any problem with payments.

The equity you invest in your home is a valuable resource. It can finance improvements to your current domicile, increasing its value, and it can be the means for a down payment on your next home. These are excellent uses of equity that have major benefits down the road.

The bottom line on home equity loans is that they can be used as original debt or to help pay off existing debt, much as a debt-consolidation loan. What do you do with your credit cards once you've paid off the debt? See the preceding section for "desist and destroy" instructions.

Step 2—Shorten your payment schedule.

The faster you get out of debt, the less you pay in overall finance charges. In addition, as money is freed up and available for investment, it will be working productively for you. The idea of reducing your monthly payment or payments can be seductive, but if you're forced to continue making those payments month after month, what have you gained? If you decide to consolidate your debt, don't be lured by the fool's gold of low monthly payments; be concerned instead about how quickly you can get your debt paid off.

Step 3—Get rid of credit cards.

We've said it before, and at the risk of sounding like common scolds, we'll say it again. Get rid of your credit cards. Perhaps it's not feasible to destroy all your cards, but you certainly can live without those charging exorbitant interest rates.

However old-fashioned it may seem, learn to use cash. There's something magical about using cash. You're not so quick to part with it. Even paying by check or debit card doesn't impose the same sort of caution and discipline as parting with cold, hard cash. Using cash will make you a better budgeter and planner.

Step 4—Build up financial reserves as you pay off your debts.

Managing your debt efficiently is our goal here, but it's easy to get too aggressive. Don't assume you can apply all your excess income to debt retirement. You'll never get out of debt if you don't start to build some reserve for the items that got you in debt to begin with. The usual suspects are repairs and maintenance for home and autos, vacations, gifts, and clothes.

No matter how focused you are on debt management, you should be setting money aside every month for these irregular expenses. After all, making sure you don't have to borrow money to pay your plumber or auto mechanic is a way of debt management as well.

Mortgaging your home...without mortgaging your life

Dubious as we are about debt, we do recognize that most of us need to borrow for our major purchases—home and cars. Owning a home is the American Dream; the opportunity to own spacious homes, without sharing them with other families, is one of the distinguishing characteristics of our society. To that we say: Go for it, but be mindful of your other goals as a couple.

Today, many dual-income couples have the ability to finance expensive homes at the outset of their marriages; the notion of beginning with a humble little "starter" home is considered quaint and oh-so-20th century. But large homes at the start of a marriage can be a trap.

For example, a large home may require a mortgage of 20 years, 30 years, or more. If you're planning for extensive mid-life travel, your ability to afford that may be affected by the need for ongoing mortgage payments. Or let's suppose one of you wants to quit your job to stay home with the kids. You may have enough money for your down payment, but with your joint income reduced, will you be able to make your mortgage payments? Larger homes also mean greater home maintenance costs. If only one of you is working, will the upkeep of your home be affordable?

All we're suggesting here is that you think about the consequences of purchasing an expensive home—and the trade-offs your purchase may require. That sort of balancing act is a constant as you implement and modify your budget.

Once you commit to home ownership and save enough money for the down payment and closing costs, here are other aspects of mortgages to consider:

Length of your mortgage

As with all debt, the longer the mortgage period, the more you spend on finance charges. Think about how long you want the responsibility of mortgage payments. Coordinating the length of your mortgage with your lifetime goals is a major step in achieving financial freedom. If you decide to move or refinance your existing mortgage to gain a lower interest rate, don't automatically refinance for 30 years or some other lengthy term. Keep your goals in mind. Your life together is about more than lower monthly mortgage payments.

Fixed-rate mortgages

A fixed-rate mortgage locks you in at a specific interest rate for the length of the mortgage. There is security here; you know that your interest rate won't change. This certainly will help in your budgeting.

However, be aware that if your payments for property taxes and homeowners' insurance are bundled into your mortgage payment, you may see an increase in the total package over time if those other elements increase.

As you consider fixed-rate mortgages, compare the difference in monthly payments between a 15-year mortgage and a 30-year mortgage. Many people assume, incorrectly, that the monthly payment on a 15-year mortgage is double that of a 30-year repayment. Because the interest is lower on a 15-year loan and the repayment period is so much shorter, the monthly payment may be surprisingly affordable.

Adjustable-rate mortgages (ARMs)

As the name suggests, interest rates with ARMs are subject to change. The triggers for adjustment, which are specified in the mortgage agreement, typically are changes in certain financial measures, such as the prime rate or cost-of-living index. Because ARMs typically offer lower interest rates than fixed-rate mortgages, they can be attractive. But you may be in for a ride on the rate roller coaster that can frustrate budgeting and present you with unexpectedly large payments later on.

Here's a good tactic for dealing with the uncertainty. If your agreement provides an overall cap on your interest rate (or a cap on the increase in any year) you can plot out the maximum you would pay. Can you afford it? If not, it's farewell to ARMs.

When renting makes sense

In the long run, most of us are better served by owning our homes. We're investing equity that we can use as a financing tool, we can create the sort of living environment that we want, and we have some reasonable expectation of being able to sell our homes at a profit. Owning a home can be a major step on the road to financial security.

For all that, homeownership is not the best option for all couples. Consider those who expect to relocate frequently. As homeowners, they would be subject to closing costs and fees—and possibly realtors' commissions—with each sale and purchase of a home. And, because they would be occupying their homes for a short period, there would be no guarantee that their domiciles would appreciate in value. It's quite possible that in this situation, couples could take a financial beating by owning their homes.

There are many good reasons for owning a home, but sometimes, the reasons for not owning one are more compelling. If you're in that situation, you shouldn't feel like second-class citizens for renting. That's simply the best option for you.

The real deal on wheels

In the best of all worlds, convenient, affordable, and timely public transportation would chauffeur us to our jobs, our recreation, and any other places we elected to go. It may happen some day, but for now, few of us live in communities with public transport jewels. For most, cars are a necessity. That means borrowing for automobile purchases and upkeep (and budgeting for same) are necessities as well.

In the age-old debate about buying versus leasing, we come down firmly on the side of buying. Leasing commits you to a perpetual car payment, and who needs that? On the other hand, financing a car is a losing proposition because cars are a depreciating asset. Not only does the value of your car decline every year, but you're also paying interest on the money you've borrowed. Owning a car may be a necessity, but it comes with a big price tag.

Our advice on autos is to own a car, take good care of it, plan on keeping it for eight to 10 years or until repair costs become excessive, then purchase a new one. Here are some other "Rules of the Road" on auto financing:

Rule 1—Buy a used car with a good warranty.

This enables you to avoid the major depreciation hit that comes in the first two years of new car ownership. With a used car, the previous owner suffered the depreciation blow.

Rule 2—Finance a car for the shortest period possible.

Your auto is a depreciating asset; the longer you pay for it, the more money you waste.

Rule 3—Never finance a car for longer than it's covered under its "bumper-to-bumper" warranty.

When things begin to go wrong and you must pay for repairs, even as you're making loan payments, you could be on a long downward spiral. Also, be wary of "extended warranties," especially for used cars. These warranties typically are not "bumper to bumper" and contain many exclusions tucked away in the small print.

Rule 4—Leasing works in certain circumstances.

If you simply must have a new car before you pay off your old vehicle, a lease could make sense for you. Typically, when you trade in a car with a loan balance, the car is rarely worth what you owe for the new vehicle. Therefore, your buddy Smilin' Jack just rolls over the remaining balance onto your new car loan, creating a debt snowball that is careening downhill. If you do lease, pay attention to the terms of the lease and mileage allowances.

Rule 5—Save now for your next car.

Once you pay off your car loan, don't go on a spending spree with the money you're saving. Instead, establish a car fund and contribute each month the money you were paying for your car loan. That way, you can pay cash or make a larger down payment for your next car, eliminating the need for a loan or substantially reducing its size.

Paying down debt: the delicate dilemma

As we close our discussion of debt, we must address one of the more delicate dilemmas of modern marriage: how to handle debts each of you may have accumulated before the nuptials. Years ago, such a discussion hardly would have been necessary. People married young, well before they had accumulated significant debts—or assets, for that matter.

Today, the opposite is often true. When people wed today, it may be after a decade or longer as professionals, plenty of time to borrow plenty of money. The same is true of people in second or third marriages. It would be hard to imagine people in that situation without some debt burden.

When couples bring individual assets to the marital table, that's a cause for joy. When the baggage includes debts, the issue is more complex and more volatile.

Broadly, there are two approaches you can take to pre-marital debt. You may decide to reduce your debt as individuals, or you may elect to pay down premarital debt as a couple. Each approach brings advantages and disadvantages.

Paying down premarital debt as individuals can prevent conflict, particularly if one party incurred substantially more debt than the other. With this approach, the partner with the smaller debt load doesn't feel financially strapped by decisions made before the marriage. This approach also permits each spouse to maintain a significant level of independence.

But there are disadvantages as well. For one, the debt might not be paid down as quickly or as efficiently as possible, because only one partner is focusing on it. In addition, that partner may feel resentment at being abandoned on Debt Island. That could promote continued use of debt, resulting in financial hardships and marital discord.

If you elect to pay down premarital debt as a couple, you can develop an efficient game plan that emphasizes quick payment of high-interest debt. You can get out of debt more quickly and focus on your goals as a couple. This joint process also implies regular communication about debt, an activity that will help you many times over.

The principal disadvantage to this approach is that the partner who kept the slate relatively debt-free may feel exploited; the good spending habits he or she developed might appear to have come to naught.

As we mentioned, this is a sensitive matter, and we don't recommend one approach over the other. What we *do* recommend is talking about any premarital debt and developing a game plan that pays off all debts quickly while keeping both partners satisfied with the strategy.

 *Pillow talk*

1. As an exercise, spread all the credit cards each of you carries on a table before you. Now, try to name the issuer of each credit card—not Visa, MasterCard, or American Express, but the bank or financial institution that issues the card—as well as the annual interest rate for each card. Loser has to call the issuers to negotiate better rates.

    Just kidding. The goal here is to make you more aware of the interest you're paying on credit-card purchases, cash advances, and transfers. Once you become more familiar with eye-popping interest rates, you're likely to exercise more caution with credit-card debt.

    It wouldn't hurt to make those calls to negotiate better rates. In today's competitive environment, you might get results that will surprise and please you.

2. Take the sample budget template on the next page and fill in the amounts you think are appropriate. In the first go-round, do it as individuals, without consulting your partner. When each of you has finished, compare notes. Are there differences in the allocations each of you has penciled in? If so, this may imply differences in goals.

    Talk about those differences. See if you can establish mutually agreeable goals and budget allocations.

    Now, fill out the budget template again, this time working together. *Voila!* Your first budget is now complete and ready for action.

Our Budget

	Monthly Expenses	Monthly Totals	Annual Expenses	Annual Totals
Employment Income				
Less:				
Payroll Deductions				
Federal Income Tax				
State Income Tax				
Social Security Tax, Medicare Tax				
Health Insurance				
401(k) Contributions (__%)				
Total Payroll Deductions				
Joint Fixed Expenses				
Rent/Mortgage				
Renters' Insurance				
Household Supplies/Maintenance				
Food				
Utilities:				
Gas, Electric, Telephone				
Cable, Internet Service				
Medical/Dental				
Life Insurance				
Total Joint Fixed Expenses				
Joint Discretionary Expenses				
Dining Out, Entertainment				
Vacations				
Unforeseen Expenses				
Contributions/Subscriptions/Dues				
Savings/Investment				
Total Joint Discretionary Expenses				
Husband-Fixed Expenses				
Car				
Transportation Costs/Maintenance				
Car Insurance				
Cell Phone				
Wife-Fixed Expenses				
Car				
Transportation Costs/Maintenance				
Car Insurance				
Cell Phone				
Total Individual Fixed Expenses				
Husband-Discretionary Expenses				
Clothing				
Personal Care Services/Products				
Hobbies/Gifts				
Unforeseen Personal Expenses				
Wife-Discretionary Expenses				
Clothing				
Personal Care Services/Products				
Hobbies/Gifts				
Unforeseen Personal Expenses				
Total Discretionary Expenses				
TOTAL EXPENSES				

Chapter 3

Ensuring Your Future (I): the Lowdown on Health, Automobile, and Other Insurance

---

When we wed, we pledge to abide by the Golden Rule. Yet marriage sometimes is guided by a radically different principle: Murphy's Law. When things can go wrong, they do. You or your partner becomes ill at an inopportune time. Your car breaks down on the Highway to Hell. Your fridge goes on the fritz, your washing machine washes out, and your VCR is R.I.P. These misfortunes range from the frightening to the merely inconvenient, yet there is a common denominator: All can be covered by insurance to minimize the impact.

When we're single, we typically don't think much about insurance. Our responsibilities may not be extensive, and we're not obliged to consider protection for a loved one. Marriage changes the equation dramatically, especially if yours is a dual-income household. Your standard of living goes up and, accordingly, your ability to maintain that standard of living now becomes dependent on the health and success of your spouse, in addition to your own.

Securing the life you now enjoy, in a cost-effective manner that provides you with sufficient protection, is an essential step on the road to financial success. Some decisions, such as those involving health insurance and automobile insurance, must be made almost immediately; you don't want to be without protection in these key areas for even a day. Fortunately, most single people already carry these types of coverage. The initial tasks of newlyweds often are to review and consolidate coverage rather than to acquire new policies.

The same can't be said of other coverage, such as disability insurance and life insurance, which typically will be considered for the first time after the marriage. Because these are such uncomfortable areas, many couples will address them by not addressing them. That is, they'll put them off until some un-specified time in the future, when it may turn out to be too late.

It would be immeasurably nicer to bask in the glow of your marriage or honeymoon without having to contemplate the illness or death of you or your beloved. But you must do it, and the sooner the better. Your lifestyle is now dependent on two people rather than one; insufficient insurance can result in catastrophic consequences.

In this chapter, we'll look at the most important categories of insurance and discuss the best ways of approaching them. (We'll save life insurance for Chapter 4. Because of its complexity, and its potential as an investment vehicle, it merits a separate discussion.)

Health insurance: whose plan...or is it both plans?

Many people receive health insurance through their em-ployers. If you and your partner are planning to remain with your current employers, you'll need to review in some detail the health-insurance plan of each employer, so that you can decide whether to maintain enrollment in both plans or switch to joint coverage through a single plan.

The health benefits situation today is as complex as it ever has been. Plans can be structured through health maintenance organizations (HMOs), preferred provider organizations (PPOs), or along other lines, and the benefits they offer can vary widely. Deductibles, copayments, and lifetime limits span a wide range, as does coverage for prescriptions, dentalcare, and eye care. Moreover, employers of a certain size are required to offer multiple health insurance options, complicating your decision still further.

As you review your current plans, consider these five key issues as they apply to you and your spouse:

The immediate health needs of you and your spouse

If you have ongoing medical needs for treatment beyond annual physicals and prescription drugs, take a close look at which of your plans offers the most cost-efficient reimbursements where your specific needs are concerned.

Availability of your current doctors

Loyalty is vital in healthcare. If you've been seeing a physician or a specialist for years, chances are you're comfortable with that professional and would willingly pay a premium for the right to continue seeing him or her. In an HMO or PPO, you may well need to pay that premium, because these plans typically limit full reimbursement to "in network" care; if you go out of network, your reimbursement may be significantly less.

So before you make any decision about changing health plans, you'll want to determine if your physician and any specialists you're seeing are in the provider network of your spouse's plan.

If your doctors aren't participants in your spouse's plan, which may look pretty attractive otherwise, all is not lost. At your request, your physician can initiate the process of becoming a participating provider in your spouse's plan. Insurers update their provider networks regularly, although it may be on an annual or semiannual basis. So with a little patience and persistence, you may end up with the best of both worlds: access to your personal physician and specialists in a superior health plan.

Treatment of prescription drugs

Although many health-insurance plans include deep discounts for prescription drugs, some also feature a catch. That is, to realize your discounts, you may need to purchase your drugs from a participating pharmacy, which could be quite inconvenient if the nearest participating pharmacy is across town, or in bulk via mail order. This is an issue of convenience as much as cost; factor it into your thinking.

Deductibles

Most plans feature deductibles, the amount for which you're responsible before your plan provides reimbursement. Where individuals are concerned, deductible amounts are roughly comparable. However, when a spouse is added to coverage, the deductible amount can rise geometrically rather than arithmetically.

Depending on your medical needs, it may be more efficient for you as a couple to have just one deductible to meet. On the other hand, if the deductible soars when a spouse is added to your coverage, it may make more sense for each of you to stay enrolled in your current plans. This is one more factor in a complicated field.

Employer-paid premiums

Rare is the employer that pays 100 percent of your medical premiums. Most often, you are required to contribute a portion each month through a payroll deduction. How much is that contribution?

How much is your spouse's contribution? And how much would your contribution be under joint coverage in a single plan?

Employee contributions often are the hidden joker in the health-insurance deck; they can rise dramatically when a spouse or children are added to a health insurance plan. Understanding these costs will help you determine the best approach for you and your spouse.

Once you and your partner study your needs and the features of your current plans, you'll be well positioned to make an informed choice about health-insurance plans. Some couples will find it more advantageous to remain with their respective plans; the coverage suits them, and it's cheaper than joint coverage in a single plan. However, if one spouse has a superior plan that better accommodates the medical needs of both of you, you may find joint coverage the way to go, even if it costs a little more.

As with most marital financial decisions, choosing the right health insurance plan involves trade-offs. In this case, however, even a handsome financial gain is unlikely to compensate for inferior medical coverage.

One final word here. No matter which health-insurance option you choose, remember to create a category for health care—and all other insurance costs—in your budget. The category should include the contributions of you and your spouse to monthly premiums (costs that are regular and predictable) as well as your estimate of costs for copayments and prescription drugs. Of course, you can't know these in advance, but if you don't plug in an estimate, you may be waylaid by unexpected medical expenses that will put your budget in intensive care.

Supplemental insurance

No matter how generous your health insurance, you will pay out of pocket for certain uncovered expenses. Because many plans typically cover less than 100 percent of medical expenses—

70 percent or 80 percent are common repayment figures—you're responsible for the balance. You'll also incur deductibles, copayments, possible out-of-network expenses, and some subtle costs, such as lost wages and transportation to and from hospitals and doctors' offices, that few plans will reimburse.

A number of firms write policies called supplemental insurance, which reimburse you for these and other out-of-pocket expenses. Whether or not supplemental insurance is for you depends on the cost of the premium versus the benefits provided, as well as the breadth of your basic plan. If your plan, for example, covers 100 percent of physicians' and hospital costs, supplemental insurance could be superfluous. But if your plan pays only a portion of your costs because you must see out-of-network professionals, supplemental insurance may be worth investigating.

One supplemental insurer, AFLAC (the folks with the duck in their advertisement), provides coverage for more than 40 million people worldwide. AFLAC's success has created many believers. In fact, when the National Association of Investors Corporation surveyed its member investment clubs in 2000, it found that AFLAC was the most widely held stock when measured in number of shares. Must be something about that duck.

Health insurance for the self-employed

According to the National Association for the Self-Employed, about 10 million Americans were self-employed in 1997—a figure that is on the rise—and thus ineligible for any employer-provided health insurance. If you and your spouse are both self-employed, medical insurance plans are available, of course. Sad to say, these generally have not kept pace with employer-provided plans in either cost or scope of coverage. Inevitably, you'll pay more to receive the same coverage (or less) enjoyed by corporate employees, and you may need to mix and match plans to achieve full coverage in such areas as dental care and eye care.

Insurers provide more attractive plans to corporations because of the volume involved; being guaranteed so many participants enables them to lower their prices. If you and your spouse are self-employed, you can try to take advantage of the same volume discounts.

Many business organizations, such as local chambers of commerce or small business associations, offer their members health insurance plans based on the same principle as corporate plans: Lots of participants equals lower costs. Large voluntary organizations, such as the American Association of Retired Persons and the National Association for the Self-Employed, tap the same concept in offering health plans to their members.

Membership dues for such organizations often are at a low or even nominal cost. The savings such group plans offer against individual plans can be so significant that you'll recoup what you pay in dues many times over.

Disability insurance: a must to protect your income

When most couples consider insurance, they know that health and automobile insurance are mandatory and that they probably should explore life insurance when they can get around to it. Disability insurance may be as vital as any other type of coverage, yet it's an often overlooked aspect of financial planning. You and your spouse might have crafted a solid financial plan and a budget that will help you achieve it. But if either of you loses your earning capacity to a disabling injury or illness, your financial plan could be rendered meaningless because your ability to contribute to it could be dramatically reduced. The scenario can be further complicated if a disability of either of you results in additional, unforeseen expenses. Quite a squeeze it can be: Your costs go up while your earnings capacity plummets.

Many of us pay scant attention to disability insurance because we know our employers are providing it. We remember that orientation session when the human-resources manager advised us that we had disability coverage and that we would notice payroll deductions to cover our portion of the premium.

Indeed, employer-provided coverage is common and appreciated. Frequently, however, it's far from adequate. It's imperative for you and your spouse to undertake a three-step process to lead you to adequate disability insurance.

Step 1—Review the disability coverage provided by your employers, with these questions in mind:

What percentage of your salary will the benefit pay each month?

Typically, disability coverage pays only a percentage of your income. If that percentage is too low, you could experience a serious income shortfall in the event of disability.

In addition, there are potential tax consequences should the benefit be paid. If your employer pays your premiums, any benefits you receive are taxable. However, if you pay the premiums, your monthly benefit is not subject to income taxes. Any tax obligation, of course, will serve to reduce the money available to you.

How long will the policy pay the benefit?

Some policies may pay for a designated number of years; others may pay until age 65. If your policy pays for only, say, two years, it's clear that you are substantially undercovered. If you're planning to work past the traditional retirement age, even a policy that pays through the age of 65 won't suffice.

How does your policy define "disabled"?

Some policies offer benefits that kick in if it's determined that you no longer can do your own job. This is called an "own-occupation" trigger. Other policies won't pay the benefit unless you're unable to perform *any* job, a much broader definition of disability that works against you, because the insurance company could refuse to pay you as long as you could work in some other field.

As you review your current disability coverage, don't be surprised if you come up with disturbing answers. The fact is that most employer-provided disability programs are inadequate for the needs of today's couple. But now that you're armed with that information, you're prepared for the second step.

Step 2—Determine your needs in the event of disability.

Not all couples have the same requirements here. To determine your needs, explore these questions with your spouse:

$ As a couple, how much money do you need each month?

$ Should one of you became disabled, how much of a shortfall would there be in meeting your monthly expenses?

$ Does your existing disability coverage, including potential Social Security disability benefits, cover the shortfall? If the answer is yes, you now know that your disability coverage is sufficient. But if, as most do, you answer no, then it's time to proceed to the final step.

Step 3—Explore a supplemental disability insurance policy.

You can achieve this through a life-insurance agent or a financial planner, and it should be a priority. The premiums are not inexpensive. Nor does a disability policy allow you to build equity, as some life insurance policies do. Nevertheless, adequate disability insurance is an important tool in planning a secure financial future for both of you.

Automobile insurance: how marriage changes the rules of the road

We don't intend to harangue you about the necessity of automobile insurance; that's what your insurance agent is for. Most people are veteran drivers with plenty of auto-insurance experience well before marriage. Many couples live in states that require auto insurance; if you're among them, you already realize that your options are limited.

But marriage can change the auto insurance issue in ways both obvious and subtle. For example, your spotless driving safety record may have persuaded your insurer to offer you a discounted rate when you were covered as an individual. But if your spouse's safety record is checkered, how will your insurer respond when you seek joint coverage? Clearly, your good-driver discount is at risk.

Other auto insurance questions you should consider follow.

Does your current policy require you to notify your insurance company of your marriage?

This may seem a small point, but your insurer has a legitimate interest in knowing if your vehicle or vehicles now will be driven by someone in addition to you, and to review and adjust your premium accordingly. If you fail to notify your insurer of your change in marital status, you could be subject to penalties and even cancellation of your policy.

Should any new vehicles purchased be titled and insured individually or jointly?

Some tricky legal issues are at play here. Let's suppose that, with a new, jointly titled car, one of you is involved in an accident and sued as a result. If the legal decision goes against you, would the joint assets of you and your spouse then be subject to attack? In the same situation, if the car is individually titled, would that protect your joint assets in any lawsuit? The answers to these questions can vary from state to state, so good legal counsel may be advisable here.

Many couples choose to jointly title all their important assets as a display of their commitment to each other. We salute that, but we also want you to be aware of the potential consequences.

Appliance insurance... and when it makes sense

We'll be the first to admit that losing your telephone service may not be as frightening as a medical emergency, but breakdowns in appliances and utilities can be an inconvenience or worse. If you or your spouse depends on the telephone for your living, to cite one example, disruption in service can be more than an annoyance.

Many providers of household appliances have developed insurance policies or maintenance contracts to protect you against breakdown, or rather to assure speedy repair, because no one can guarantee against malfunction. This category has an almost limitless number of entries. You can buy insurance for your refrigerator, washer, and dryer; maintenance contracts for your VCR and computer; and wireline maintenance agreements for your electricity, natural gas, and cable television. Not all such policies and agreements are available in every community, but they are commonplace.

If you purchase an insurance policy or maintenance agreement with each appliance or utility, the costs can mount pretty quickly. Thus, it may be wise to ask yourselves these questions before you purchase the insurance:

Is the value of the appliance worth the premium?

Unless you're some sort of Pop Tarts junkie, you're unlikely to want insurance for your toaster. It's such a low-end item that you wouldn't want to spend a nickel on repair or a maintenance agreement. Many couples would put VCRs in the same category. If you get a good few years' use from your unit, you might not want to invest in repairs; VCRs are fairly low priced, and you're probably ready for the next generation anyway.

Yet value is a relative thing. Some couples never would consider a wireline maintenance agreement for their cable TV, for example, because they view television infrequently. They can wait indefinitely on repairs. For others, cable TV might be a principal source of information and entertainment; for them, a maintenance agreement might be vital. No one can determine the value of particular appliances and utilities but you.

Who will perform the repairs, and when?

If you're buying insurance for your refrigerator, it's important to know who will provide the repairs. Will the store that sold you the product be performing the repairs or will it be a contractor of the store? If it's a contractor, does he or she have offices and personnel near you, or are you likely to have to wait several days for a technician to travel from afar? You'll want to know the answers to these questions.

Also, check the policy or agreement to make sure it imposes some sort of deadline on the insurer, such as "Repair to me made within two working days." If this commitment is lacking, the policy may not be worth much.

Are you required to ship or transport the appliance to the repair shop?

This is a fairly common feature of maintenance agreements for such appliances as VCRs and computers. Disengaging them, toting them to your car, driving cross town to the repair shop, then reversing the process once the repairs are completed—all that can be laborious and a misuse of your valuable time. A

Healthcare Cost Comparison

	Your Plan	Spouse's Plan	Your Plan (Joint Coverage)
Percent of costs paid (In network)			
Percent of costs paid (Out of network)			
Deductible			
Copayments			
Prescription drugs			
Pharmacy restrictions?			
Lifetime limit			
See your own doctors?			
Dental care included?			
Dental deductible			
Dental annual limit			
Eye care included?			
Key limitations?			

better alternative may be to find a reliable technician who's willing to make on-site repairs. Even if you pay a premium for those services, you'll recoup it in hassle-free time.

 *Pillow talk*

If each of you currently is covered under an employer-provided health insurance plan, you have three choices for the future: remain enrolled in both plans, enroll jointly in your plan, or enroll jointly in your spouse's plan. This exercise should help you understand the benefits and advantages of each option.

With all your health plan documents before you for quick reference, work together to fill out the chart on this page. When you're done, you'll have a better understanding of the strengths and shortcomings of each option and a better feel for your spouse's concerns and priorities.

However, even with all the blanks filled in, your selection may be far from obvious. You may find, for example, that the lowest-cost option won't permit you to see your own doctors except by paying a stiff out-of-network penalty or that it suffers from what we call a "key limitation," such as a low annual cap on reimbursement for mental health treatment. The chart and the corresponding discussions with your spouse should help make you both aware of the trade-offs.

Profile

Audrey R. Korotkin and Don C. Clippinger:
Where the Turf Meets the Torah

An award-winning writer and editor, Don Clippinger has covered horse racing and the thoroughbred industry for more than two decades.

Audrey Korotkin is rabbi of Temple Judea Mizpah, a 350-family Reform congregation in Skokie, Illinois. Their occupations may appear to make them just about the unlikeliest couple anywhere. But in this case, when the turf meets the Torah, the result is a solid union based on the principles of mutual respect and joint planning.

Prior to their marriage in 1989, both already had distinguished careers in journalism and public relations. Don's previous marriage contributed to a mature perspective.

"We were both older adults who had been living on our own for a long time," Audrey confirms. "It's not like we didn't know how to run a household. We both came with a mature attitude to financial matters. That was very helpful."

What wasn't helpful was an unexpected jolt to their employment status.

Don had successful stints in various editorial positions with the *Pittsburgh Post-Gazette* and the *Philadelphia Inquirer,* and in 1988 he became editor of *The Thoroughbred Record,* the industry's oldest trade magazine. Audrey, an award-winning news and sports reporter at WBAL-AM radio in Baltimore, had been executive director of Triple Crown Productions. But just after their marriage, they both found themselves out of full-time work and starting their own PR business serving primarily the racing industry.

When they jointly decided that Audrey would attend rabbinical school—the five years of study would feature an exciting but expensive year in Israel for Audrey—they knew the road ahead might be difficult. But the business that Don now runs, Kilbourn Associates LLC, has thrived, Audrey is established in her temple and a leader in the community, and the lessons in frugality and partnership they learned during their challenging early years together continue to provide benefits.

Communication

When Audrey counsels young couples planning to wed, she firmly guides them to a policy of full and regular communication. Thus, it's no surprise that Audrey and Don practice what she preaches.

"Our discussions are more or less continual rather than structured," Don reports. "We've always talked things through."

Checking accounts and credit cards

Maturity, mutual trust, and joint planning are themes that run through this marriage, themes that are reflected in the couple's approach to checking accounts and credit cards. They maintain two joint checking accounts; one account is for household expenses, the other for variable and unexpected costs.

"We both know what's going in and what's going out," Audrey says. "There are never any surprises, never any secrets."

As for credit-card debt, they have none.

"We eliminated that," Don says, "although we both had pretty much cleaned the slate coming into marriage."

Asset consolidation and titling

Audrey and Don each had an IRA account; both changed the beneficiary to reflect their new status. Since their marriage, Don also invested in a 401(k) plan while he was managing editor of another trade magazine, *Thoroughbred Times*. Audrey's assets included profit-sharing benefits from the Triple Crown Productions job. Each created a rollover IRA, with beneficiary properly designated, for these assets.

Budgeting

Of necessity and choice, they've adopted a formal approach to budgeting. A portion of Audrey's income is paid in a "parsonage" allowance; for that, Audrey and Don must maintain comprehensive records of all expenses related to housing and home upkeep. It's a great head start on budgeting.

"We sort of have the budget in our heads rather than sitting down and writing it," Don says. "We do the mental calculations—this is the housing nut each month, these are the recurring payments. That pretty much takes care of us."

Their budgeting goes well beyond the expenses associated with the maintenance of their residence.

"We sit down every week and plan out our meals and any extraordinary expenses for the week or even month ahead," Audrey says. "We do a lot of our shopping together. We're blessed to have similar temperaments and priorities. When one thinks it's important to spend money, usually the other does, too."

Advice for newlyweds

$ **Don:** "The thing that worked for us is getting rid of credit-card debt. That meter runs at 20 percent a year. I know it's tough to avoid it when you're starting out, but streamlining your finances opens up the vistas of investment and retirement planning."

$ **Audrey:** "As a rabbi, I require premarital counseling of couples planning to marry. Other than religion, money is one of the biggest sticking points in a relationship. If one's a saver and one's a spender, it's a real serious problem. If you don't share information about the debts you're bringing to the relationship, that also can be very serious.

"A lot of couples try to put it aside; they think they'll work it out sometime after they get married. I'm very insistent on counseling, even with older couples. I might broach the subject differently, but I think it's important that they discuss financial issues now and not afterwards."

Investments and long-term goals

Because they're so adept at living within their means, Don is able to set aside a significant amount each month for contribution to his pension fund. In addition, the temple provides Audrey with a pension plan, which is overseen by a board of rabbis.

"We do have a chance to review allocations every year," Audrey says.

The couple also has engaged professionals to help them acquire disability insurance for Don and provide advice on investments beyond their pension plans. Their current vehicle of choice is mutual funds.

All these investments are elements in a master financial game plan. Although many couples have trouble planning for even a month or two ahead, Audrey and Don have mapped out a strategy that calls for them to work for 20 years, then retire on the strength of their investments.

"Retired rabbis have a lot of opportunities to do what we do on a freelance basis," Audrey says, "One of my mentors who has retired is officiating at Rosh Hashanah and Yom Kippur services in Hawaii. Passover cruise ships are always looking for rabbis."

Don, who is an active participant in Audrey's congregation, would gladly go along for the ride.

Chapter 4

Ensuring Your Future (II): Preparing for the Worst

We've all seen the commercials. It's a sunny day, the birds are singing, all's right in the world, then—whap!—the Big X smacks you and you're gone, deceased, an exparrot, out of the picture. What's worse, the grim-voiced narrator reminds you, is that you could be leaving your loved ones without enough resources to continue on after you.

You may find those cheery messages to be heavy-handed, offensive, aggravating, or all of the above. But, boy, are they effective. We'll wager that the first time you actually gave serious thought to life insurance was when you viewed one of those doomsday prophecies. Each time we see one, we're tempted to call our agents and instruct them to double our coverage. Nasty as they are, these commercials drive home an effective point. You or your spouse might not be around to enjoy that secure financial future you're planning for yourselves, so it's the job of both of you now to prepare for that scenario.

As we discussed in Chapter 3, insurance is about protecting yourself and your standard of living from unforeseen,

potentially tragic circumstances. Clearly, the loss of a spouse falls into this category. Life insurance is among the best methods of guaranteeing the financial future of the surviving partner.

Think about your current financial situation and your spending priorities. You're in the process of building your lives together, making major purchases that typically include a house, cars, and furnishings. You're in an accumulation phase, with perhaps little money left over for savings. This is when your insurance needs are as great as they'll ever be: You simply lack the assets to sustain your lifestyle if confronted by a catastrophic event.

Later in your marriage, life insurance might not be so urgent (although you still should consider it for estate planning purposes, as we'll discuss later in the chapter), because you will have accumulated sufficient resources to tap if tragedy strikes. Your children will grow, your debts will be paid, and your financial responsibilities will ease. So you no longer may need the protection that life insurance provides.

But for now, you and your partner should spend serious discussion time on life insurance, so go for it. Here's the two-step process that we suggest.

Step 1—Discuss your needs.

In your discussion, focus on these key questions:

Would the surviving partner want to maintain your current residence?

A painful question to be sure, but one you must explore. There are practical and emotional issues here. You may be attached to the residence you shared with your spouse and wish to remain there no matter what the cost. Yet by yourself, you might not need as much room as you once did; if you remain in your current domicile, you must pay for the upkeep of your big house. These costs must be factored into your life insurance needs.

It's just as possible that the surviving spouse might want a smaller home. Selling your house would provide you with a cash infusion; moving into a new home would require a down payment and ongoing mortgage and maintenance costs (or rent) if you choose not to own. The deliberations are tricky, but you must consider all your housing needs and costs.

Would the surviving partner continue to work?

If so, that would produce continuing income that life insurance would not need to provide. But if the surviving spouse likely would retire, that would mean loss of a key income source; the death benefit of a life insurance policy could help make up the difference.

How much time would the surviving partner take off work to complete the healing process?

Loss of your loved one is devastating, so crushing that most people require a considerable time before they're ready to again face the world of work. If you think that healing time for you might be measured in months, you'll need to include the lost income in your computation of life insurance needs.

What debts would the surviving partner need to pay off?

This is one of the most difficult needs to project; you can't possibly know what financial obligations you might undertake over the coming years. Perhaps more than any other question, this one underscores the need for constant marital communication. If each of you plans to maintain a relatively high level of financial independence, you'll need to communicate regularly about what debt you may be incurring. The last thing a surviving partner needs is the shock of unexpected financial obligations.

How much monthly income would a surviving partner need to sustain the desired standard of living?

Your monthly budget should be a handy guide here. If you adjust the income and expenses according to your answers to the previous questions, you'll have a pretty fair sense of the financial needs of the surviving partner.

Step 2—Find a trusted professional to help secure your coverage.

When you sit down with your life insurance professional, you'll be way ahead of the game. Unlike most people seeking life insurance, you'll know exactly what you need from your policy.

Armed with the information you supply, your agent will prepare a future value calculation to determine the lump sum of money necessary to generate the income the surviving partner would need, as well as the corresponding premium.

When you reach this point, you'll have done your job well, but your work doesn't end here. Acquiring the right life insurance begins with understanding your needs, but those needs will change over time. If you raise a family, shift jobs or careers, buy a new home, or inherit money, your expectations of life insurance may change. Update your coverage as needed. If you think of your approach to life insurance as a dynamic process rather than a one-time purchase, you'll be able to accommodate all the changes in your life.

Types of life insurance

We've been discussing life insurance as if it's a one-size-fits-all fashion, with variations only in the amount of the death benefit and corresponding premium. In recent years, the insurance industry has introduced a variety of products that, at first blush, may be confusing. To cut through the clutter, think of these two broad categories of life insurance:

Term insurance

As the name suggests, term insurance covers a specified length of time. One year would be a common period for a policy. After that term expires, your policy is subject to renewal and adjustments in premium. With term policies, premiums typically are based on your age; the older you get and the more of a risk you are, the higher your premium is likely to be.

To add a degree of predictability to your premiums, you can opt for a "level term" policy that covers a lengthy period, perhaps 10 or 20 years, and keeps your premium level throughout.

Perhaps the key thing to remember about term insurance is that there is no cash value once the term expires. Your premiums are not invested for you. What you get for your payments is the protection of the death benefit, but no money beyond that. Because term insurance lacks an investment component, it's usually the most inexpensive type of life insurance available.

Permanent insurance

We'll use this catchall phrase to describe policies designed to provide coverage for the long term. Permanent insurance comes in various forms: whole life insurance, universal insurance, hybrid term/whole life insurance, and variable insurance are just some of the wrinkles developed by the industry.

No matter the type of permanent-insurance policy, the common denominator is that these vehicles invest your premium payments to build cash value for you. The uses for your gains are many. Some couples use the cash value to finance their children's education, or they draw upon it as retirement income. Others allocate their gains to offset their premium payments.

A key feature of these policies is that your money grows on a tax-advantaged basis. That is, you pay no income taxes on the money as it accumulates.

Premiums for these policies typically are higher than those for term insurance.

Which is the best policy for you?

Should you select an inexpensive term insurance policy or a more costly permanent insurance policy that builds financial value? The answer depends on your current financial status as well as your goals for the future. How much can you afford to pay in premiums? Do you have other investment vehicles that may obviate the need for permanent insurance—and its expense? Your answers to these questions will help you determine the right policy for you. Also, consider these potential purposes of life insurance:

Income replacement

If your primary need is to replace lost income upon the death of one of the partners, term insurance may be the most suitable option. Often, you can coordinate your policy with major financial events in your marriage or: Your children have finished college, your mortgage is paid off, you've built a little nest egg. With a little savvy on your part, your policy can expire just when your need for income replacement declines significantly.

Investment purposes

The idea of using life insurance to accumulate wealth seems attractive, but it's no slam dunk. You always need to compare the costs and potential gains of permanent insurance against the other broad option: eschewing permanent insurance and investing the money you would have paid for premiums in some other vehicle or vehicles.

In some cases, investing through a life-insurance policy is not as efficient, due to the cost of the insurance and the overhead of the insurer. On the other hand, if you need life insurance coverage, are in a high tax bracket, and may be facing an estate-tax liability, permanent insurance may be the best option.

Estate planning

In estate planning, life insurance is used as a gifting vehicle that can reduce the amount of estate shrinkage due to taxes. Here's the way it works. Ordinarily, a large estate bequeathed to your children can trigger significant inheritance, income, and estate taxes that can prove quite onerous for your beneficiaries. However, you may gift assets to your children through a life insurance policy; within well-defined limits (no more than $10,000 gifted to any recipient in any year) there are no gift taxes for your beneficiaries. For this option, couples typically use a permanent life-insurance policy with a "second to die" clause. That is, the children receive the benefits only after the deaths of both spouses. (Beyond life-insurance, gifting assets to your children usually is a sound practice. It reduces the current and future size of your estate while easing the tax burden for your beneficiaries.)

The gifting feature of permanent life insurance can be a big plus for your children, and it can work for you as well, if your parents have significant assets they intend to pass on to you. Through life insurance, they have the opportunity to gift part of their assets directly to your children, rather than magnifying your potential estate-tax problems. If you're in this situation, it might be a good idea to involve your parents in your discussions about life insurance.

One cautionary note. If you and your parents are considering this option, you'll want to pay attention to an obscure provision of the tax code called the "Generation Skipping Tax," which can be triggered when assets are transferred beyond one generation. The Economic Growth and Tax Relief Reconciliation Act of 2001 provides for the eventual repeal of this tax. In the meantime, don't skip it; discuss it with your tax preparer or financial planner.

(We'll discuss estate planning in greater detail in Chapter 12.)

Employer-provided life insurance

Many companies offer life-insurance coverage as a benefit for their workers. The premium typically is inexpensive, so inexpensive that it's almost impossible to pass up. Yet there are risks in relying on the coverage your employer provides.

First, you lose control of your life insurance plan. If you and your employer part company—and in today's economy, that's the norm rather than the exception—or if your employer decides to alter the benefits provided, you and your spouse may find yourself without appropriate coverage. In addition, if you wait until your next job to seize control of your coverage, you may be older and not as healthy, and coverage could be more expensive as a result.

It *is* a good idea to take advantage of whatever life insurance coverage your employer provides, but it's a bad idea to rely on it exclusively. Think of it more as an add-on, an enhancement to the coverage you and your spouse plan and acquire. That way, changes in job or employer never can jeopardize your coverage.

Plan a healthy lifestyle

If you're considering life insurance for the first time, be aware that most insurers will require you to undergo a medical examination to assess your physical condition. They'll also query you about some personal habits, including whether or not you smoke cigarettes and how often, and your medical history, including past and current diagnoses, prescription drugs you're using, and doctors you're seeing.

The results of the exam can be a major factor in your premium. For instance, if your health is poor and you smoke several packs of cigarettes per day, not only will your premium be high, but you actually could be deemed uninsurable.

The healthier you are, the lower your premium is likely to be. In more ways than one, staying healthy may be the best life insurance for you and your spouse.

 *Pillow talk*

Once you've determined your life insurance needs, and you're committed to life insurance as a vital component of your financial planning, you'll need to identify a professional to help you. In most communities, the life-insurance field is crowded. How do you find the right agent? We've discovered that an old-fashioned technique, word of mouth, works well here.

Survey your family and friends about their agents and coverage. Each of you should keep notes on your findings as the basis for a family discussion about life insurance agents. When you've narrowed the field to the most promising two or three candidates, don't hesitate to follow up by asking your friends more specific questions about their coverage and agents.

When you contact the top candidates, you'll find them eager to visit your home or office and to prepare a proposal for you. Be sure to get at least several proposals from different agents for comparison. Remember that what they're presenting to you are proposals, not final offers. Ask questions. Request modifications. Negotiate. This is an important transaction for you and your spouse, and you want to bring to it the same tools you utilize in a business deal.

Chapter 5

Investment Planning: Getting Up Close and Personal with Risk

You've developed a workable budget, and you've taken steps to protect your income against unforeseen setbacks. If we think of these as the defense measures in marital financial planning, it's now time to take the offensive to achieve your financial goals. By this we mean investing.

Investing is the aspect of financial planning that provides you with the wherewithal to enjoy life to the fullest and accomplish your most cherished goals. You've considered these goals before, of course, as you planned your budget and insurance coverage. But now that you'll be investing part of your hard-earned income towards the achievement of your goals, it's the appropriate time to prioritize and refine your objectives.

As a couple, it's critical for you to spend quality time discussing your goals. The process itself is uplifting. When you evaluate and pursue investments as a couple, you establish yet another bond between you. You're a team of two against the world, so to speak. The impact on your marriage could well be unmatched.

At this point, the more conservative among you might ask: "Why invest? We have two incomes and a plan to live within our means and keep us in our comfort range, so why shouldn't we put some money into savings accounts and certificates of deposit and avoid the risks of more aggressive investing?"

The answer is a simple one. In our economy, it's risk that's rewarded to a much greater degree than talent or hard work. Few couples will achieve their financial dreams if those dreams are financed by income alone. It may seem harsh and unfair that your abilities and industry generally will bring you only modest rewards, but it is a fact in the society we've constructed. Of course there's risk in investing, but the greater risk may lie in not investing. Let us show you what we mean with an example.

Consider Couple A, who have implemented a conservative, risk-averse investment plan. Their excess money goes into safe vehicles, such as bank accounts and CDs, which give them an average annual return of 5 percent. If Couple A invests $200 each month, after 20 years, their total investment of $48,000 will grow to approximately $83,100.

Now, contrast that scenario with that of Couple B, who have mapped out a more aggressive investment program that features both greater risk and an average annual return of 10 percent. Over 20 years, their investment of $48,000 will grow to approximately $154,600—$71,500 more than Couple A's nest egg. The same amount of money was invested, but it was invested more productively.

Think of what that extra $71,500 means. Couple B will have an easier time financing their children's college education. They can retire earlier if they choose, travel more if they choose. And they can relax, because they know they have enough in reserve to cover any circumstance that may arise.

This is not to diminish the risk that Couple B endured or the risk to you if you invest aggressively. There is risk, and you could lose all or part of your investment. But as we say, there are risks to not investing proactively as well. Let's examine the types of risk involved with both the aggressive and conservative approaches.

Market risk

This is the risk that people fear most—and with some justification. Invest in the stock market and there's a chance, however slight (unless you're investing in inherently unstable companies), that you'll lose your entire principle. Those who analyze the market regularly have refined the concept of market risk. They think of it as "principle fluctuation." In this more advanced definition, the key concern is not loss of the entire principle but the degree of fluctuation your investment will experience on a day-to-day basis.

In other words, each investment you make brings what might be called a "risk/return" relationship. Generally, the more risk (or volatility) you can accommodate, the greater your potential return. Otherwise, there would be little payoff for taking on the uncertainty.

When we speak of market risk, we mean the price fluctuation of an investment based on the overall economy and conditions, not necessarily the financial stability of any one company in which you may have invested. Sluggish consumer spending, poor performance of the market in general, disappointing showing by a particular sector—all are market risks that can affect any of the stocks in your portfolio. Even upside market momentum can create risk. We witnessed this in the late 1990s when some investors assumed that the stock of any dotcom would skyrocket. When the bubble ultimately burst, even fundamentally sound companies—and their investors—suffered the consequences.

As has been demonstrated in recent years, volatility is a characteristic of the market that's unlikely to change. If you choose to invest in the market, you and your spouse will need to determine your tolerance for significant market swings.

Credit risk

Unlike market risk, which entails the general direction of the stock market in the face of changing economic conditions, credit risk involves the financial stability of individual companies in which you might invest. Businesses that aren't making money or are carrying significant debt on their balance sheets often present a high degree of credit risk.

It would seem to follow that investments in unstable companies have major downside potential. Some investors, however, seek out such companies on the theory that the greater the risk, the greater the potential return. Buy the stock of an obscure, no-profits start-up, this theory goes, and you'll be in on the ground floor when the company takes off. This type of speculative investing in technology and Internet stocks was the rage in the late 1990s. Investors in dubious dotcoms soon learned that they weren't on the ground floor at all; they had many more levels to fall.

Credit risk also is an issue when buying individual municipal and corporate bonds. Analyze the financial stability of the issuer, and don't think that corporations or municipalities are immune from collapse. When California's Orange County defaulted on its municipal bonds in the 1990s, it demonstrated the perils of credit risk pretty persuasively. And don't be lured by higher interest rates; with bonds, the relationship between risk and reward is clear and direct. The higher the interest rate, the lower the quality of the bond.

Inflation risk

Market risk and credit risk, of course, are perils associated with aggressive investing. But there also are dangers related to passive savings. One of these is the peril of inflation. It's one of the most important factors that you must understand when establishing your financial goals and game plan.

Simply put, inflation represents the decline in purchasing power of your money. Because of inflation, $100 that you spend today will not buy the same amount of goods and services five years from now. If you do the grocery shopping for your family, you well know the meaning of inflation. You're spending much more for the same amount of food than you did even a few years ago. That's the power of inflation.

Apply this same lesson to your financial planning and you'll get an alarming sense of the risk of inflation. Let's suppose that your income need today is $40,000 per year and that you want to retire in 25 years. If we assume an average annual inflation rate of 4.8 percent—the actual average over the past 25 years—your annual income need 25 years from now would be slightly more than $129,000. And that's assuming that your needs won't change, which is a risky assumption at best. If you don't incorporate inflation into your financial planning, you're not likely to get where you want to go.

Think of it another way. If the average annual inflation rate is 6 percent, and your conservative investments are earning an average annual return of 5 percent, your purchasing power is declining by a rate of 1 percent per annum. You're not actually losing money, but you might as well be, because your purchasing power is dropping.

The legendary economist Adam Smith coined the term "invisible hand" to describe the unseen but powerful controlling factors in a free market. Were he around today, Smith might called inflation the "invisible hand in your pocket." You can't see it, don't feel it, but it's picking your savings pocket nonetheless.

Interest-rate risk

Just as inflation can adversely affect seemingly conservative, safe investments, so too can the roller coaster of interest rates. An illustration: In the late 1980s and early 1990s, investors in certificates of deposit were on top of the world, enjoying annual interest rates of 8 percent to 10 percent. Many CD holders were able to finance retirement from their interest gains alone.

Then the economy turned upside down, and CD interest rates dropped dramatically, to 3 percent or lower in some cases. Those new retirees found themselves with an unappetizing set of choices. They could research other, more aggressive investments—and it was pretty late in the day for that—or they could swallow hard and accept a reduced standard of living.

The fact of the matter is that swings in interest rates can be as unpredictable as changes in the stock market. Nor are CDs the only investment vehicle affected by moody interest rates. Bond mutual funds, to cite another example, can be directly and adversely influenced by changes in interest rates. When interest rates rise, bond valuations decline. The reverse also is true. Decreasing interest rates bring increasing bond valuations.

Imagine you own a bond paying 6 percent, only to find that soaring interest rates increase the payout rate of newly issued bonds to 7 percent. If you try to sell your 6-percent bond, you'll be forced to reduce your price. If you don't, investors will ignore your offer and purchase newly issued bonds at the more attractive 7-percent payout rate.

From this discussion, it should be clear that risk is a feature of all investment. Trade-offs are inevitable. If you aren't able to come to terms with market risk, you'll expose yourself to a greater degree of risk from inflation and fluctuating interest rates.

Which risks are right for you? Determining that should be a product of your investment planning.

Setting time frames for your goals and investments

Once you understand the types of risks associated with various investments, you're better able to factor those risks into your investment planning. Yet another consideration in selecting investment options is the time frame associated with each of your goals. Some of your objectives are immediate; still others are envisioned for many years into your marriage. The timetables you establish for achievement of those goals can affect the investment options you choose.

We find it best to divide goals into those that are short-term, to be achieved within the next five years, and those that are long-term, which won't be realized until at least five years out. The purchase of a home would be considered a short-term goal: You expect to accomplish it within five years. Because automobiles need to be replaced regularly, their acquisition should be viewed as a continuous short-term goal. Most other large annual expenses, such as family vacations, also are short-term goals.

Long-term goals would include saving for your children's education, purchasing a second home, and financing your retirement.

As you group your goals into short-term and long-term, think of how risk can affect your ability to achieve them. For example, if you plan to finance your children's education, a long-term goal, through such conservative investments as CDs, inflation could significantly diminish the buying power of your investment over time, and you may fall short of rising tuition costs.

On the other hand, if you're thinking of financing that hot new sports car, a short-term goal, with your gains from a market investment, even a brief downturn in the market could rob you of principle as well as projected earnings.

In the next chapter, we'll explore the many investment options available to you and help you understand how to match investments to your short-term and long-term goals. Some people have a predisposition for certain investments and a reluctance to consider others. When you've finished the chapters on investment, we hope you come away with the readiness to utilize any investment option that will help you achieve your goals.

 *Pillow talk*

1. As a couple, review your financial goals. Include everything: goals you hope to achieve over the next year or two as well as goals you've established for a lifetime. When you have your list of goals, designate each as either short-term or long-term. Keep this list handy. We'll consult it as we begin to discuss investment options.

2. We've somewhat jokingly called inflation "the invisible hand in your pocket," but the impact of inflation is no laughing matter. To demonstrate just how painful inflation can be, try this exercise.

Take out your budget; the annual figure represents your income needs for one year. (If you use a monthly budget, annualize it. That is, multiply your monthly spending by 12.) Now, take that figure and multiply it by 1.5981; this represents what 10 years of inflation at 4.8 percent will do to your income needs. You haven't purchased one additional item, haven't added a nickel to your spending plan, yet your income needs likely will increase by almost 60 percent over the next decade.

Don't despair. As you'll learn in Chapter 6, there are ways to make up the difference.

Chapter 6

Investment Options...
and Plenty of Them

Investment options...they're everywhere. They range from the stock market, perhaps the best known of investments, to bonds, to commodities futures, to insurance, to pension funds, to individual retirement accounts, to certificates of deposit and passbook savings accounts. If you start a business or buy into another person's enterprise, you're investing. Purchase the contract of a professional golfer or bowler in the hope that your athlete will win plenty of money for you? That's investing.

Or you may elect to stuff your money in a big, boxy mattress. That's investing, too, although not the strategy we would recommend. Gold, land, rare coins, art, stamps, baseball cards—all can be used as investments. In fact, just about anything you purchase and hold, with the expectation of appreciation in its value, can properly be called an investment.

Many would-be investors find the sheer number of choices so overwhelming that, in effect, they opt out, selecting only the most conservative vehicles. That may have been you once

upon a time, but no longer. You and your spouse have a workable budget and a firm sense of where you're going financially, and you've established a comfort level of risk. Now you're ready to dig deep into investments and choose those that will best meet your risk tolerance level while advancing your goals.

Throughout our book, we've been stressing the importance of spousal communication and joint development of goals and plans. In investing, this team approach becomes even more vital. No two people have precisely the same tolerance for risk. Inevitably, one partner will be more aggressive, the other more conservative. Communication may not help you eliminate or reconcile any differences in investment philosophy. But regular discussions will help you forge a mutually agreeable approach. That way, when your investments succeed, you'll share the credit. If any investments fail, you'll shoulder the blame jointly rather than engage in the recriminations—"I told you there was no future in Susan B. Anthony dollars!"—that can poison a marriage.

A number of gender-based studies have suggested that, when it comes to investing for the long term, women are more successful than men. Women do their homework up front and are able to deal with the roller-coaster ride of investing; men tend to make changes, sometimes too frequently, sometimes too impulsively.

These are broad, perhaps overbroad, generalizations that might not apply to your marriage. But there is a valuable lesson here for those with pronounced investment tendencies. If patience is your chief virtue, by all means exercise it, but don't be so averse to change that you miss opportunities to improve. On the other hand, if you tend to be quick on the investment trigger, modify your impulsiveness a bit by slowing down to review all options.

In addition to discussing goals and risk tolerance with your spouse, it's important that each partner begin your investment journey with a comprehensive understanding of your current financial situation. Each of you needs to know your assets—what they are and where they are—as well as the names and contact numbers of any accountants, brokers, insurance agents, financial planners, attorneys, and other professionals who may be advising you. It wouldn't hurt to commit all this information to writing; a couple of neat pages should do it.

You go to these lengths to document your assets and advisors, of course, in case one spouse, due to the death or disability of the other, is placed in the unfamiliar position of handling family finances. In that situation, ready access to your financial information is critical. If you try to track down and understand this data during a period of peak emotional distress, you may not make the best decisions.

Those are the preliminaries. Complete them and you're ready for investing. In guiding you to the best investment approach for your marriage, we'll begin with the broadest perspective and consider investment categories and the various ways you can participate. In Chapter 7, we'll go inside the categories and explore investment products, how they should be structured within a portfolio, and how you and your spouse can combine assets that each of you brought to your glorious union.

Major asset classes

As noted, the number of investment options is almost limitless. With rare exception, however, investments fall into one of three categories: cash, fixed-income, and equity. Let's take a look at each.

Cash assets

Cash assets are those investments that are readily accessible, experience no price fluctuation, and, therefore, pose no risk to principle. Examples of cash assets would be checking accounts, savings accounts, and our old faithful: a mattress stuffed with greenbacks.

Cash assets are the safest form of investment, at least in terms of risk to your principle. However, there is a serious trade-off involved with cash assets. What you gain in accessibility you lose in return, which is negligible or nonexistent. Checking accounts sometimes pay you interest, at a modest rate, for the slight inconvenience of maintaining a minimum balance. Savings accounts may pay a little more than checking accounts for the added inconvenience of not being able to write a check. The mattress doesn't pay anything; squirrel away $1,000 and that's exactly what you'll fish out come that rainy day.

Cash assets pose no market risk, but they're hardly risk-free, as you'll be courting the dual dangers of inflation and interest-rate fluctuation. For example, if your passbook savings account is paying 3 percent and inflation is running at an annual rate of 3.5 percent, you're actually losing purchasing power, especially after the government takes its fair share of income taxes on any interest you earn. And that 3 percent return you're enjoying isn't guaranteed. Changes in interest rates, which may occur at any time, can reduce your return.

Fixed-income assets

These investments offer a fixed rate of return for a specified period of time. Typically, they feature some kind of guarantee to principle if owned for that entire length of time. The guarantees may come from government agencies, such as the Federal Deposit Insurance Corporation (FDIC), or from corporations or other private-sector organizations.

In addition, some investment vehicles composed of fixed-income assets (such as a bond fund) don't provide guarantees to principle because the bonds may be traded.

Many types of organizations issue fixed-income investments. Among them are:

$ **Banks.** Banks issue certificates of deposit. CDs usually are backed by the bank and the FDIC, up to total deposits of $100,000 with the issuing bank.

$ **Government.** Uncle Sam provides fixed-income investments in the form of treasury securities. These pay a fixed return for a specific period of time and are backed by "the full faith and credit of the U.S. government"—legal jargon with which you'll become familiar if you invest in fixed-income assets.

$ **Municipalities.** Municipalities issue bonds to help underwrite such projects as highway improvement, school modernization, and other civic initiatives. These bonds are backed by the full faith and credit of the municipality; that's okay as far as it goes, but financial strength among municipalities can vary. As a result, most municipal bonds are evaluated and rated by such independent professionals as Moody's Investors Service and Standard & Poor's. The best grade is "AAA," and the ratings descend from there. In some cases, municipalities acquire insurance coverage for their bonds to provide additional safety for investors; investors pay a price for this protection in the form of lower interest rates.

To encourage this type of investment, the federal government and the states in which the bonds are issued exempt from income taxes the gains from certain municipal bonds.

$ **Corporations.** Much like municipalities, corporations issue bonds to help finance expansion and improvements. Corporate bonds are backed by the full faith and credit of the corporation; as with municipalities, these instruments are rated by independent services to help investors understand the financial stability of, and risk associated with, the issuing company. The same risk/return principles apply: The safer the bond, the lower the interest rate. The riskier the bond, the greater the possible return.

Fixed-income assets are popular investments, as they promise some return with apparently minimal peril to your principle. Yet there are risks involved. Bonds, for example, are only as secure as the organizations that issue them are stable. Invest in a bond and you become a creditor of the issuing organization. You're lending them money that you hope they'll pay it back, along with a handsome premium. But the issuing organization could falter or fail, taking your investment with them. Thus, it's wise to consider the following questions about fixed-income assets:

If you're investing in bonds, when do those bonds mature?

The maturity period for bonds may be as long as 30 years. Try to cash in early and you could suffer a significant loss of principle (the exact penalty will be specified in the prospectus). In addition, the amount you get back with an early cash-in could fluctuate with changes in the market value of the bond. If you intend to finance short-term goals through bond proceeds, make sure the maturity periods are consistent with your goals.

If you've chosen CDs for your investment, are you comfortable with the interest rate?

CDs lock up your money for an often-lengthy period at a designated interest rate. A CD with a 10-year maturity period could pay you 5-percent interest each year for the next decade. But what if interest rates next year rise to 7 percent? Will you be comfortable with your lower rate for the next nine years? Better to answer that one up front.

Equity assets

When you invest in equity assets, you're taking ownership in the underlying asset. In fact, you can think of "equity" and "ownership" as interchangeable terms. The most common form of equity asset is the stock of publicly held corporations. Buy a share of stock and, in essence, you're purchasing a piece of that company, albeit a small piece.

Generally, equity investments can be expected to provide a greater return than fixed-income investments, and here's why. Unlike creditors, equity owners use their debt to create more opportunity and strengthen the enterprise. When all is said and done, after repaying the debt and sweetening it with interest, the organization has created more value than the cost of the resources.

It's not much different than considering a home-equity loan to finance your household improvements. If the projects don't add enough value to your home to at least cover the amount of the loan, it would not be a wise financial decision.

Thus, equity assets provide a means for higher investment returns. But the fundamental risk/return principle doesn't vary. Where prospective returns are greater, so too is risk. Unlike fixed-income assets, stocks don't provide a guaranteed return for a set period. The value of your asset could grow or diminish. To become a successful owner of assets, you must consider what you're buying much more carefully than with other types of assets.

Let's return to the example of your home; real estate also is a form of equity asset, by the way. When you're scouting homes, you consider many factors: location, structural soundness, energy efficiency, and future marketability.

Selecting stocks entails the same careful study you would devote to the purchase of a home. You should consider the company's financial stability, its competitiveness, its ability to keep and grow its market share, its share price relative to its earnings, and its potential future earnings. Although many investors are adept and comfortable performing this type of analysis, others are not. If you're among the latter, check out our discussion of financial advisors in Chapter 8.

Mutual funds

In the minds of many, the stock market is the very epitome of risk. Watching the progress of your investment is like viewing an oscilloscope: You're getting moment-to-moment feedback from the heart of your financial strategy, a nerve-wracking experience when the path turns downward. Your distress can be aggravated if you invest in, say, a single company's stock. If that company hiccups, your sole investment could be jittery as well.

Mutual funds can help you relieve that dependence on a single or a few corporations. They're offered by many investment companies, which aggregate the funds of participants in one big investment pool. Although all mutual funds share that same basic approach, their investment targets vary.

Bond mutual funds, for example, invest in bonds, but they're even more narrowly targeted than that. Government bond funds invest in government bonds, corporate bond funds in corporate bonds, and so on. On the other hand, stock mutual funds invest in stocks. They may target specific industry sectors—utilities, healthcare, and technology—or they may seek stocks that pay dividends or those with high-growth potential. All mutual funds publish a prospectus, a detailed document that specifies the fund's investment objectives and provides background about the fund.

For many, mutual funds are the investment of choice. They offer these advantages:

Professional management

Each mutual fund has a professional money manager, or team of managers, researching hundreds of individual securities and making buy-sell decisions. Whether it's analyzing the financial stability of a municipality for a bond fund or the growth potential of a technology start-up for a stock fund, this is what professional money managers do full-time. Because typical investors never would have the time or inclination to produce such research and expertise on their own, chalk up professional management as a huge advantage for mutual funds.

As a potential mutual-fund investor, you should take responsibility for one research task. Become as familiar as you can with fund managers, including their experience and any investment tendencies. A fund may have a great long-term track record, but if the manager responsible for that track record no longer is there, the performance history may be less relevant.

Diversification

Mutual funds typically invest in a large number of individual securities. In many cases, stock funds and bonds funds own well more than 100 different securities. This diversification can reduce your overall risk dramatically. If you have $10,000 ticketed for investment, would you feel more comfortable buying two different stocks only or acquiring a piece of a portfolio with 100 different stocks? No investment is completely secure, but in this game, there is safety in numbers.

Flexibility

Flexibility is another decided strength of mutual funds. They allow you to invest with a small initial stake, and they make it easy for you to enhance your investment or withdraw funds. Invest in a single bond and your cash is locked in for many years. Invest in a bond mutual fund and you get diversification and the ability to make withdrawals.

Picking the right class of assets

We all know people who have developed a, shall we say, fondness for certain investment classes. They're always bullish on the market, or they love bonds, or they wouldn't be caught dead in CDs. This lack of flexibility is precisely the wrong way to go about selecting the right asset classes for you. What's the right way? Simply match the asset categories to your needs and goals.

Remember that the riskier an investment, the more the price fluctuates on a daily basis. The more the price fluctuates, the more time you need to allow the investment to work through its cycles and provide positive results. With that understanding as a foundation, here's a useful set of guidelines for applying asset classes to your financial game plan. (It might be helpful to reference your list of short-term and long-term goals as you go through the guidelines.)

When to use cash assets

Use these for short-term purposes. If you know you'll need the money in 12 to 18 months, this is the safest place for your cash. You'll also have access to your money for unforeseen expenditures that may arise. (We're thinking here of a new hot water tank, not a junket to Las Vegas.)

When to use fixed-income assets

These investments will generate a higher return than cash assets and should be targeted for intermediate-term goals—objectives you'd like to accomplish over the next 18 months to three years, such as purchasing a new car or home. Fixed-income assets also provide some stability for money that you don't want to invest in the stock market. Even if their goals are long-term, many investors would be uncomfortable with all their money in the market. Fixed-income investments are your safety net. However, over the long haul, we know that equity investments should outperform fixed-income assets.

When to use equity assets

As noted, this category offers the greatest long-term potential, as well as the most risk and price fluctuation. Some so-called experts believe they can help you "time" the stock market ever so precisely—jump in when its at its ebb, hop off when it peaks. You heard it here first: Timing the stock market in this manner is an impossible task. No one consistently predicts turns in the market with a high degree of accuracy. If they could do it, market gurus wouldn't be hustling how-to newsletters and books. They simply would do it, retire to their own private islands, and, as they sip piña coladas, not lavish another thought on you.

Instead, let's apply sound asset-allocation principles to make equity investing work for us. Aside from investing in quality stocks, time is your key ally. It makes sense to compare the time frame of your key goals to the past performance of any investments you've targeted. This will give you some indication of the potential risk and volatility within a sector.

For example, if you're considering a fund comparable to the S&P 500—a very broad, inclusive index of stocks—and your time frame is more than 15 years, your risk of principle loss is virtually eliminated. As your time frame shortens, the risk and volatility level increase. With equity assets, time is on your side.

Investing *is* for you

If we haven't persuaded you yet about the necessity of investing, let's go one step further with a concrete example that applies to many families: saving for a child's college education.

Let's assume your youngster will attend college for four years, beginning in 2019, and that college costs will increase an average of 6 percent per year. For that education, you'll need to come up with $162,326 for a typical nonprivate school.

One way to approach that cost is to hope Junior becomes a child star and pays his own way. That failing, you're stuck with a $162,326 bill.

College Savings Comparison

	Investment Return	
	4%	10%
Average Annual Cost of a Public Education	$13,000	$13,000
Estimated Annual Inflation Rate	6%	6%
Estimated Total Cost of Education	$162,326	$162,326
Years Until College	18	18
Monthly Investment Required for 18 Years	$513	$268
or		
Lump Sum Investment Today	$80,129	$29,196

Or you can invest. You can reach that $162,326 goal by investing $513 per month at an average annual return of 4 percent. If you get even bolder and enjoy an average annual return of 10 percent, it will take a monthly investment of $268 to reach your goal. You also could try to do it all now through a lump sum investment today; it would require $80,129 with an average annual return of 4 percent, $29,196 with that average annual return at 10 percent. The table above illustrates these paths to financing college education.

As they say in the auto repair industry, you can pay me now or pay me later. Paying it now, through monthly investments, seems a lot less painful, doesn't it? By investing in productive vehicles, you can improve your ability to achieve your most cherished financial goals. Not by getting a second job, not by scrimping, not by sacrificing, but by doing some homework and investing properly.

 *Pillow talk*

We know you and your spouse are perfect for each other, but are you investment-compatible? That is, do you have the same general philosophy when it comes to investing your money? Now is the time to find out.

Following are several investment-related maxims. Your job is to complete them with the choices, from the options listed, that seem best to you. Your answers might suggest how you feel about investing, as well as your tolerance for risk.

There are no right or wrong answers. Rather, the questions are designed to elicit your approach to investing—and any gap between you and your spouse in these matters. If there is a gap, don't be discouraged. Rather, discuss your differences. Resolve those you can, and live peacefully with those you can't.

1. It's wise to abandon an investment whenever the principle loses:
   a. 5 percent
   b. 15 percent
   c. 25 percent
   d. 50 percent
   e. Don't abandon it. Things are bound to get better.

2. When the value of your investment appreciates, it's best to sell when the gain reaches:
   a. 5 percent
   b. 15 percent
   c. 25 percent
   d. 50 percent
   e. Don't sell. We're on a roll.

3. The proper amount to invest each month is:
   a. $0
   b. $50
   c. $100
   d. $250
   e. $500

Profile

Sarah and Sam Miller: Personifying the Joys and Challenges of Modern Marriage

You won't meet a more delightful couple than Sarah and Sam Miller—open, gregarious, comfortable with each other and with the world at large. Each has an interesting and rewarding career that provides well for them and Sarah's 18-year-old daughter Debbie, who soon will begin college.

Sam is a professor of engineering at a prestigious university, and he supplements his income with an unusual specialty: providing expert court testimony on such esoteric matters as patent infringement for certain intellectual property and personal injury cases.

Sarah's career began inauspiciously; as a student at George Washington University, she typed death reports for an insurance company. Today, she is a respected therapist with specialties in art therapy and eating disorders. She's written a book, currently being reviewed by publishers, that will help sufferers of eating disorders overcome their denial and identify and treat

the ailment. (Because of the sensitive nature of Sarah's practice, we've changed the names of this family and omitted the name of the city where they live.)

With their income, they've renovated their home; helped finance Debbie's music lessons, private schooling, and precollege film course at New York University; and enjoyed frequent traveling to such locales as China, Thailand, South Korea, Italy, France, Spain, Mexico, Ecuador, and Guatemala.

They've had it all, it would seem, but they've paid a price. As Sam somewhat ruefully notes: "Ever since we've been married, we've been spending more money than we've been taking in."

Credit-card debt and income tax obligations have forced Sarah and Sam to tap their savings and refinance their home.

"Despite having this huge wake-up call, we still don't have a budget in place," Sam says.

As the couple has reached their 50s, something new has crept into their equation: nagging doubts about financing their retirement.

"It was easy to not be honest and deal with the fact that we're trading off our future for our present, which isn't a good thing," Sam says. "Now, I'm concerned about how we'll stay afloat in retirement. I guess I'll work until I drop."

Communication

To listen to them openly discuss their differing views on clothes—Sarah favors frequent purchases, Sam prefers to wear them out—is to understand that this is a couple that has taken the ego out of joint planning. There's no topic they won't take up as a team, and no discussion that engenders any resentment, no matter how frank the exchange.

"Our situation works really well because we trust each other," Sarah says. "I've never felt threatened, never been afraid that Sam would take our money and do something behind my back."

Asset consolidation

In his 40s when he and Sarah wed, Sam had accumulated assets in the form of stocks. These remain individually titled, although they've been drawn down to meet debts.

"If I'd just left that money in the market and done nothing with it, we'd have a lot more now," Sam allows. "Using it is too easy. It's all kind of abstract, just numbers on a ledger."

Budgeting

Repeated raids on their assets prompted the couple to review their financial situation a few years ago. The news wasn't good.

"I concluded that we were overspending by about $1,000 a month," Sam reports. "At first when I ran the numbers, I didn't believe it. But I watched the numbers over a six-month period, so I couldn't claim there was a short-term fluctuation. So I knew we were running in the red."

Despite that revelation, the goal of budgeting remains elusive.

"The real question is, can we buckle down and budget, and stay within that budget?" says Sam. "We say we can, but until we do...."

Checking accounts, credit cards, and bill paying

They maintain separate checking accounts, having tried—and abandoned—the joint approach.

"We didn't keep our assets separate deliberately," Sam says, "but there was never any particular reason to move them together. I don't understand how people manage joint checking accounts."

Adds Sarah: "I always felt it was the right thing to do, to have this joint checking account. But he'd write a check, I'd write a check, we didn't know who was writing checks, and it was just too complicated.

"Now, Sam may say to me, 'Do you have $1,000 for the mortgage?' I say, 'Sure, here, take it,' and I write out the mortgage check. But if I'm at the end of my account, I'll say, 'Can you pay for Debbie's lesson?' and he says, 'Sure, no problem.' It's always been like that. Whoever has more money writes the check, and we don't count who paid for what."

They've been attempting to rein in their credit-card debt, with some success.

"Over the last few months I've been trying not to use the credit card," Sarah says. "I write checks so I can track everything, and I use the credit card only in emergencies."

Taxes

As a self-employed professional, Sarah must pay estimated income taxes each quarter. This, along with credit card debt, is what the couple calls "the black hole" of their finances.

"It's been the biggest source of economic distress," Sam says. "We try to say, 'We're not making all that money, we're making 60 percent of that money, we have to put that other 40 percent aside.' But the temptation to spend it is too great."

Investing and long-term goals

Although the couple has been spending more than they're earning, they haven't ignored planning for long-term goals. They invested in the renovation of their third floor and now lease it as an apartment, generating valuable additional income.

Sam also has a pension plan through his employer, an account that has grown substantially. The problem: Without cash on hand to contribute to the plan, he's been unable to take full advantage of the employer-matching feature.

Advice for newlyweds

As with most aspects of their marriage, the counsel Sarah and Sam offer for newlyweds reflects both the great rewards and financial concerns that marriage has brought them.

$ **Sarah:** "You need to trust the person you're with. That's really the bottom line. If you don't have that trust, no matter what financial arrangements you work out, they'll be problematic. You must communicate, and if you're having problems, if you're uncomfortable with what your partner's doing, you need to discuss it. That's a good marriage."

$ **Sam:** "The most important thing is to be clear about what you're spending and what you're making. Budget, and try not to spend more than you make. I know that sounds totally obvious, but in 15 years we've never been able to do it ourselves.

"Sit down and run a budget for a couple months and see where you really are. It's easy to convince yourself that every expense is temporary, that it won't recur, and use that as your rationalization. You're only deluding yourself. You have to be hard on yourself, even obsessive, with your budget."

Chapter 7

How to Marry Your Money: What to Do When Each of You Brings Financial Assets to the Union

hen people married younger, there was little need to consider the financial assets brought to the marriage. Often, those assets included little more than wedding presents and perhaps a dowry-like gift from the folks. But Grandma's wedding dress or favorite shawl didn't present any serious financial planning issues.

Things have changed, haven't they? When they wed today, couples are likely to have logged at least a few years—sometimes many years—in the workforce, plenty of time to have accumulated assets. How those formerly individual assets should be combined and held as a couple is a matter for regular discussion between you. The ramifications are many and not always pretty, as they involve thinking about the unthinkable: potential disability or death for one of you. Nevertheless, you must consider these issues related to the consolidation and titling of your assets:

Accessibility

When you title your assets jointly (that is, you place them in both of your names), each spouse will have access to the assets and can transact business accordingly. It makes a great deal of sense for each of you to have access to your savings and investment accounts, especially if you're sharing bill-paying responsibilities.

Disability

If one spouse becomes incapacitated, assets held individually cannot be directed by the other spouse without proper legal documentation, which may involve a frustrating amount of red tape, money, and time. And when you're trying to cope with this traumatic situation, time is vital.

One way to address this potentiality, of course, is to make sure that each spouse has access to sufficient assets, so that those that are individually titled aren't needed as urgently. Another approach is to provide each spouse with power of attorney for the other in the event of incapacity. Let's suppose, for example, that you as the healthy spouse determine that it's necessary to sell your home to provide cash for your new needs. Because your home most likely is jointly titled, its sale ordinarily would require signatures from both of you. With the power of attorney, you can move as quickly as you like to dispose of the house without having to jump through any legal hoops.

These approaches aren't mutually exclusive. Even if you think each of you has sufficient access to assets in the event of a health catastrophe, some assets, such as retirement accounts, can be held by an individual only. With the power of attorney, the healthy spouse can gain access to that category of asset.

Protection against lawsuits

Jointly titling your assets is a strength in some situations, a liability in others. Protection against lawsuits falls in the latter category.

This may seem an odd issue for you to ponder as you begin your marriage, but in our litigious society, it's a timely concern. Doctors, lawyers, and other professionals are vulnerable to malpractice lawsuits. Journalists can be sued for libel or invasion of privacy. Those with employment contracts always are scrutinized and sometimes sued for violation of those contracts. Throw in the unpredictable legal action that could involve any of us—culpability in a traffic accident, for instance—and you get a sense of the growing risk from litigation.

The message here is simple. All jointly titled assets are exposed in the event of a judgment against either spouse. On the other hand, assets titled individually—in your name, let's say—can't be grabbed in the event of a judgment against your spouse. And of course, your spouse's individually titled assets aren't at risk if you're judged guilty in a lawsuit.

Your degree of exposure to lawsuits should help you determine how to title your assets. If either of you works in a profession where the risk of litigation is great, this becomes an even more critical issue.

Death

An unappetizing prospect to be sure, but how property is titled not only dictates who will control assets while you're alive, but it also can provide assurances that your assets will be transferred smoothly to your heirs upon your death. Titling your assets and designating appropriate beneficiaries also will help in the management of income and taxes associated with bequests.

Make beneficiary designations a top priority, if for no other reason than marital stability. A friend of ours was married for more than three years before he designated his wife as the beneficiary on his life insurance policy. Asked why he finally made the change, he responded, "My wife would have been really upset to find out that my college roommate was getting all the money." For the sake of marital longevity, here's hoping she never did find out.

Titling options

As we've seen, how assets are titled can have significant consequences. The process becomes even more complicated for couples marrying later in life: more assets, more issues. In addition, if the newlyweds have children from previous relationships, titling issues are vital for ensuring that assets are directed properly.

The options are more complex than joint or individual titling. There are nuances here, as well as laws that vary from state to state. Here's a look at your choices:

Individual name

Where assets are individually titled, only the person listed on the accounts has access to the accounts; only the person listed on the accounts can transact business in the accounts. At death, these assets will pass through the titled spouse's estate and be distributed according to the will or via a "transfer on death" designation (see page 108) set up with a financial institution. If there is no will the assets are distributed according to the intestacy rules in your state; in many states, the surviving spouse gets one-third of the assets, with the remaining two-thirds distributed to children and grandchildren. Without proper planning, the surviving spouse may be left with insufficient assets to meet financial needs.

Although you always may opt to add a person's name to assets that currently are individually titled, the government may consider that a gift (depending on the amount) and require payment of gift taxes and the filing of an appropriate tax form. The good news here is that the government permits unlimited gifts between spouses, so you can transfer to each other as much money as you want without gift tax consequences.

Some couples adhere doggedly to the principle that all assets should be jointly titled, thinking that it reinforces their relationship and doesn't appear to put either partner in a dominant or subordinate position. If that's your philosophy, we salute you. But you must be aware of the ramifications of joint titling.

A critical factor is the capital gains tax as it applies to inheritances. This is a work in progress due to the newness of The Economic Growth and Tax Relief Reconciliation Act of 2001, which changed the equation significantly. Here's how it plays out.

Between now and 2010, if you inherit assets, you receive a "stepped-up" cost basis when you sell the assets. This means that your cost basis (the figure used to calculate your capital gains and corresponding taxes) is the value of the property on the deceased's date of death. This can be a huge benefit, especially if the asset had appreciated since its original acquisition. If that original cost was the basis for your capital gains taxes, you'd be paying much more due to the greater appreciation of the property.

For example, let's say that Person A buys a house for $20,000 and dies 30 years later when the house is worth $200,000. If the house is sold immediately for $200,000, for capital gains purposes, there is no gain and therefore, no captial gains tax. If a stepped-up basis was not available the heir would pay capital gains tax on $180,000 (sale price $200,000, less $20,000 cost basis).

However, when assets are gifted to spouses, which is what a transfer into joint name would be, the beneficiaries must assume the original cost for their portion of the assets. They don't get a "stepped-up" cost basis on the amount gifted to them. This principle is broadly misunderstood, but the consequences can be enormous.

In discussing this important federal law, we also should note that, beginning in 2010, the "stepped-up" basis for inherited assets will apply only to the first $4.3 million for spouses, the first $1.3 million for others. Remember, these provisions apply only when inherited assets are sold.

The bottom line here is to recognize that reduced capital-gains taxes for your heirs can be a solid reason for individually titling assets, particularly where those assets have appreciated substantially. But individual titling brings its own set of concerns. As we noted previously, a will and power-of-attorney documents will help assure that your individually titled assets will be directed as you wish in the event of your disability or death.

Joint tenants with rights of survivorship

This option provides the greatest access for each partner but can be somewhat restrictive. You can direct the financial institutions where these assets are held as to whether one or two signatures are required for certain simple transactions (writing checks, for example). However, more complex transactions, such as gifting stock to a third party or terminating the account, always require both signatures. As we've said many times, money is the primary source of marital conflict. If you have functioned independently but now need your spouse's approval for financial transactions, you could be courting that conflict through this arrangement.

If you title assets this way, upon the death of one of the joint owners, the balance of the assets is transferred automatically to the surviving spouse. This will happen regardless of any stipulations in the will; titling takes precedence over wills. As a result, this approach to titling can present problems if there are children from previous relationships who might reasonably expect an inheritance. On the plus side, the cost basis for computing capital gains taxes upon sale of the assets is affected for the surviving spouse. As outlined previously, 50 percent of the asset receives a "step-up" in basis.

If you and your spouse have assets titled in this manner, 50 percent of the value would be exposed if one of you were sued. Therefore, if one partner is more likely than the other to be sued, you may want to consider titling at least some assets in the name of the less vulnerable spouse. If you go this route, try to develop a defensible rationale. Should a court determine that you've transferred assets solely to shield them from a legal judgment or settlement, it could strike down the transfer, leaving your wealth as exposed as before. And you'll have a judge angry with you to boot.

Joint tenants in common

In this structure, each joint tenant is assigned a percentage of the asset. Although these assets function as joint accounts, either joint tenant may sell his or her portion without authorization of the other tenant. At death, the assigned percentage of the decedent's portfolio becomes part of the estate and is distributed to heirs via the probate process.

Joint tenants by entirety

This type of titling is available in a limited number of states and applies only to certain types of property. The advantage of this approach is that it designates the asset as "entirely" belonging to each person. Thus, it offers protection for assets as long as both tenants are living. Creditors can seize the assets only if the nonindebted spouse dies first. Should the indebted spouse die first, the assets pass automatically to the surviving spouse; there are no assets remaining for creditors. Again, this strategy cannot be used solely to avoid seizure.

Transfer on death accounts

With the exception of Louisiana, New York, North Carolina, and Texas, all states allow financial institutions to offer "transfer on death accounts," which can be used for assets titled individually, assets titled to joint tenants with rights of survivorship, and assets titled to joint tenants by entirety.

These accounts allow you to designate beneficiaries to inherit the underlying assets; probate is avoided, and the transfer of assets to you heirs goes smoothly. But there is an important caveat. In the case of assets titled to joint tenants with rights of survivorship, the assets would pass to the heirs only upon the death of the second spouse. In the intervening period between the deaths of the spouses, the designation of beneficiary is subject to change. It's our judgment that a will or trust may provide more security and flexibility than this type of account. Avoiding probate is nice, but not at the expense of family harmony.

Community property states

In community property states (Arizona, California, Idaho, Louisiana, Nevada, New Mexico, Texas, Washington, and Wisconsin) all assets acquired during the marriage are deemed to belong equally to each spouse. Individual titling in these states does not separate assets.

If you reside in one of these states, you may want to explore prenuptial and postnuptial agreements to specify marital and premarital assets. This becomes particularly important if your marriage involves children from previous relationships, children you may want to accommodate in your will through premarital assets. We'll dig into prenups and postnups in Chapter 13.

Retirement accounts

As you consider the titling of your assets, it's important to be aware that retirement accounts can be owned by, and titled to, individuals only. However, if you own a retirement account, you are permitted to name a beneficiary. This designation will supersede any stipulation in your will. For example, if your parents are the designated beneficiaries of your 401(k) account, but you specify in your will that your spouse is your sole heir, it's Mom and Pop who end up with the 401(k) cash. The moral here: Designate your beneficiaries with care.

Investment products and titling

In Chapter 6, we discussed investment categories and how you can balance your investments in each category to help you achieve short-term and long-term goals. Now let's go inside those categories and examine investment products and the titling options associated with each.

Bank accounts

From the time we earn our first allowance and learn about saving money, the bank is our first contact with financial management. Banks are popular for many reasons. Because they typically maintain neighborhood branches, they provide us with convenient access to our money. Plus, they're safe, although it must be noted that not all accounts or investment vehicles are protected equally.

Bank accounts typically are insured through the Federal Deposit Insurance Corporation (FDIC), which protects deposits up to $100,000. However, banks have taken advantage of a more relaxed regulatory environment in recent years to offer stocks, bonds, and mutual funds to their customers. These more sophisticated investment vehicles generally are not FDIC-insured. Only your deposit-type accounts (checking, savings, and certificates of deposit) are insured to the $100,000 limit.

How you title your bank accounts will be a reflection of your earlier decisions about who will manage each account. If you've decided on a single joint account, it follows that the account will be jointly titled. If you opt for one account managed by you, one managed by your partner, and a third that you both manage, then you'll have two individually titled accounts and one jointly titled account. Deciding on the number and control of bank accounts is the tough part here; titling choices are easy.

We do recommend that you establish a relationship with a bank. It could help reduce your banking fees while providing you with a partner when you need a mortgage loan or business financing down the road.

Investment accounts

Included are brokerage accounts, mutual fund accounts, and stock reinvestment accounts. All are used for investment and all may feature a combination of stocks, bonds, and mutual funds.

In titling these assets, be mindful of the implications of the federal capital-gains tax upon the eventual sale of the assets. If you add your spouse's name to an account that's currently individually titled, upon your death, your spouse won't receive the "stepped-up" cost basis on the amount gifted. Thus, if an individually titled investment account has appreciated significantly since its original purchase, it may be best to leave the title as is.

Individual retirement accounts (IRAs)

Depending on your circumstances and eligibility, you may have accumulated IRAs—traditional IRAs, Roth IRAs, IRA Rollovers—prior to marriage. Now that you are wed, we suggest that you revisit the eligibility and deductibility of contributions for both spouses. The table that follows should help. IRAs are an efficient way to accumulate retirement assets. Because IRA earnings typically are tax-deferred or even tax-free (in the case of Roth IRAs), you should incorporate these vehicles into your overall financial plan whenever possible.

IRAs must be individually titled. Because IRAs pass to your heirs via a beneficiary designation, it's important to review and modify your beneficiary designations now that you're married, especially if your beneficiary is your college roommate.

Also, remember that designating your spouse as beneficiary will not give your partner control of the account in the event of your disability. As we've noted, power of attorney documents will be helpful there.

401(k) plans

In recent years, 401(k) plans have become the investment of choice for retirement savings. If you and your spouse have access to this type of investment product through your employers, you can enjoy a number of benefits. First, you're investing with pretax dollars, so you don't pay federal income taxes on the amount invested. In addition, taxes are deferred on any income your 401(k) accumulates. Finally, many employers will match your contribution to the account, although employer contributions typically are capped.

These plans are a terrific tool for accumulating retirement savings; use them to the greatest extent possible, even if your employer doesn't match. Here are some steps to follow to maximize the impact of your 401(k) (or other plans with similar structure and opportunities but different names):

Determine how much money you can afford to contribute.

Some 401(k) participants decide to contribute only the amount each month that their employers will match. Do that and you miss out on the full benefits of this investment vehicle. Remember: You're making your contribution with pretax dollars, which will moderate the impact on your net income.

Here's a concrete example. Let's say you can budget $200 from your net income each month for your 401(k). Your $200 allocation, assuming an overall 30-percent tax bracket, actually would be structured as a $285 pretax contribution. Your net income still takes only a $200 hit, yet your account is $285 richer. The difference of $85 would have been paid in taxes had you actually received that $285 in salary. This is a perfect example of how a 401(k) will work for you.

If you and your spouse are eligible for different 401(k) plans, compare the features of each.

After you review both plans, you may decide to continue participating in each. But if one plan matches and the other doesn't, your choice may be simple.

Individual Retirement Account Comparison

	Roth IRA	Traditional IRA	Non-Deductible IRA
Maximum Annual Contribution	2001= $2000 2002-2004 = $3,000 2005-2007 = $4,000 2008 = $5,000 After 2008 = indexed for inflation	Same as Roth	Same as Roth
Tax Implications	*Not Tax-Deductible *Tax-Free Growth *No Required Distribution date	*Tax-Deductible, within income limits *Tax-Deferred Growth *Required Minimum Distributions at 70 1/2	*Not Tax-Deductible *Tax-Deferred Growth *Required Minimum Distributions at 70 1/2
Income & Employer-Sponsored Plan Eligibility	*Eligible under $150,000 *Phase-out between $150,000-$160,000 *Employer-sponsored plan participation allowed	*No limits if neither spouse participates in employer-sponsored plan. *Both spouses participate: full deductibility up to $51,000. Phase-out up to $61,000. No deduction over $61,000 *One spouse participates: full deductibility up to $150,000. Phase-out up to $160,000. No deduction over $160,000	*No income or employer-sponsored plan limitations.

Explore the loan features of each plan. We don't ordinarily recommend borrowing from your 401(k), but we also know that extraordinary circumstances can make extra cash essential. For those situations, you'll want to determine which plan offers more flexible access to your money.

Review the asset allocation of each plan.

One of the key goals in your investment strategy is balance. If you discover that your plan and your spouse's plan invest in substantially the same stock or bond groups, you may want to terminate participation in one of the plans, then use the money you had been contributing to acquire assets that will diversify your holdings.

Review your beneficiary designations and change them as necessary.

Now that you're married, be sure to designate your spouse as your beneficiary. This is a key step in working together for a secure financial future.

Monitor your investments within
your 401(k) and make changes as necessary.

After they've established their accounts and determined their monthly contributions, many participants pretty much forget about their 401(k) plans. Because contributions happen automatically, it's easy to become a passive participant. That's not what you want to be.

These plans typically offer a broad range of investment options. It's up to you as a couple to select the investment vehicles, monitor their performance, and reallocate your money as your investment strategy may dictate. Be aware and active as a 401(k) participant and always be cognizant of the goals of asset diversity and long-term success.

401(k) plans from previous employers

If you change jobs, you may be leaving a 401(k) behind. You need an action plan to ensure that you realize the full benefits from your former plan, and that the funds you've invested don't float along without proactive management. Your options are:

Take a distribution.

This is not the course of action we recommend, as your distribution will be subject to taxes and an IRS penalty of 10 percent. In addition, to ensure that the IRS gets its tax cut, 20 percent of the distribution is withheld automatically.

Roll over your money into your new employer's plan.

This is a better option, because you'll avoid taxes and penalty, but you'll be limited to the investment selection of your new plan.

Roll over your money into an individual IRA.

This option offers the most flexibility. You decide how to invest your money, without limitation.

Clearly, marrying your money involves a complex but critical series of decisions that you must make as a couple. For ease of management, it appears that jointly titling your assets makes the most sense. Yet that can increase both the tax bite and exposure to seizure in legal judgments.

Because of the complexity of this subject, we'll revisit it in Chapter 12 when we discuss estate planning.

 *Pillow Talk*

Get together with your sweetie and make a master list of all your assets. Include everything, from the tiniest checking account to the most sophisticated fund. For such investments as mutual funds and 401(k) plans, be sure to probe inside those vehicles for the individual bonds or stocks that compose the fund or plan holdings. Also, make sure you include those assets that each of you may have brought to the marriage, as well as those assets in which you've invested jointly.

When you have your master list together, you're ready to answer these three questions about your investments:

- $ Where beneficiaries are called for, have you designated the right heirs?
- $ Does your investment mix provide you with the diversity you need to build long-term growth and protect you from sharp downturns in any one sector?
- $ Are your assets titled properly? That is, does the current titling provide you with the best tax advantages; the best protection against seizure, disability, and death; and the easiest passage to your beneficiaries?

If your answer to any of these questions is no, you may need to rework your titles and beneficiaries and consider a diversification strategy for your assets. Repeat this process annually and you'll stay on the course you've charted to financial security.

Chapter 8

Do It Yourself or Use a Financial Advisor: Which Is Right for You?

When it comes to managing your finances, it's easy to feel overwhelmed. The number of investment products can be daunting. Add to that the cacophony of voices—financial newspapers and magazines, on-line investment and trading services, investment gurus holding seminars in your very town—and you get something approaching sensory overload.

One of the first steps to successful financial management is to clear your mind of the clutter. We're not suggesting that you ignore financial media; these can be valuable sources of information. But remember that these folks are reporters, not advisors. The data they provide can help you make informed choices, but the key decisions are still yours to make as a couple.

What are those key decisions? The most basic questions are these: Are you interested in, and capable of, planning your finances by yourselves? If not, should you seek out brokers, financial planners, attorneys, or accountants to help you? If you do

engage professional assistance, how do you know you're getting fundamentally solid, objective advice? This chapter is designed to help you answer these questions.

Begin your exploration of these subjects in the same way you address all important financial issues: with wide-ranging and regular discussions as a couple. Talk about how you managed finances as single people, and you'll each gain valuable insight into the capabilities and mind-set of your partner. You may discover that one of you has a strong do-it-yourself inclination, for example, and the other has experience with a financial advisor.

Review the successes and setbacks of your respective approaches to date. Discuss the amount of time you've spent managing your finances previously and how much time you're willing to commit in the future. Time can be a key factor in your decisions, especially if you have children now or plan to start a family soon. Researching investments requires time, and you may want to dedicate the bulk of your free time to your kids and family activities.

As you go about the business of determining the most appropriate financial-planning process for your marriage, keep an open mind about all approaches. Marriage has changed the equation for you. That may mean some modification of your style is in order.

Let's look first at some of the things you'll need to know if you're planning your financial future by yourselves.

The basics of portfolio management

We know that, as a couple, you've discussed and established your financial goals, and you're adjusting those goals as your changing circumstances may dictate. But once you've settled on your game plan, you'll need to make decisions about investing your money to help you achieve your goals. That's portfolio management: selecting your investment options, monitoring your investments, and modifying them as necessary.

The primary questions in portfolio management are: Are we making the right investment? What are our expectations for this investment, and are we accomplishing our goals? When is the right time to pull out of this investment and select another? The following principles should help you answer these questions and evaluate the capabilities of money management professionals.

Understanding investment products

Whether you're considering stocks, bonds, or mutual funds, learning how these marketplaces work is an essential part of managing money. One of the biggest mistakes of investors—we've seen the so-called pros falter here as well—is that they focus too much on the recent performance of a stock, bond, or fund and pay scant attention to the fundamentals surrounding the investment category involved. It may not be terribly original to point out that last year's losers may be next year's winners, and vice versa, yet it's amazing how often investors will forget or ignore this truism.

Many times, sound financial decisions go against our emotions. No doubt you've heard the expression "buy low, sell high." Think about the lack of emotional appeal for this venerable philosophy. It recommends that you invest when the market is going down or, in other words, jump on a ship that appears to be sinking. Savvy investors know that market declines often provide the best buys for issues that will reward them handsomely during the inevitable market rebound. Yet many investors still shun down markets.

Our advice is to avoid investment decisions based on emotion. Instead, research the history of the ups and downs of all the markets. This will alert you to investment opportunities while helping you avoid potential mistakes through emotional decisions. As you conduct your research, here are some factors to consider on the major investment categories.

Fixed-income assets

Bonds and certificates of deposit are the principal subcategories here. Both offer a fixed rate of return over a specified period of time; they are attractive enough, but there are potential shortcomings. With bonds, you'll want to probe the risk of default (that is, the issuer's inability to repay you) and any restrictions on liquidating the investment prior to maturity. With both bonds and CDs, study the potential impact on your investment of interest rate changes.

Equity investments

Valuation issues are paramount in determining the risk associated with investment in stocks. That is, you want to determine the underlying value of the stock and compare it to its current trading price. When you target a company for potential investment, find out as much as you can about the company's products, markets, growth rates, and debt. Do the same for the entire industry in which that company operates. Read annual reports, prospectuses, and other public filings of the company. The information you gather will give you a solid understanding rather than an emotional "feel," for the company.

For an object lesson in emotion-based investing, consider the great dotcom debacle of 2000. Investors fell in love with Internet stocks, driving them up to unprecedented and unrealistic levels. This type of "bubble" is not historically unique. In fact, financial historians have extensively documented "tulip mania" in Holland, and that was way back in 1636. The dotcom boom was equally unfragrant. Even the most cursory look at these start-up companies would have revealed that they were burning cash at alarming levels without any sign of profitability in their future. They were, in a word, doomed.

Greed, an emotional response, lured investors in, long after such investment made any sort of sense. Many dotcom backers suffered heavy losses, losses that could have been avoided with a rudimentary understanding of investment principles.

Mutual funds

More than any other asset category, mutual funds seem to be sold primarily on the basis of past performance. You've seen the magazine covers blaring the headline: "The Top 10 Performing Mutual Funds!" This message is as dangerous as it is seductive.

Of course there are great mutual funds, just as there are outstanding individual stocks. But the quest for the best is illusory, because the performance of mutual funds can be inconsistent over the short term as the sectors in which they invest come in and out of favor. Go beyond the hype and become familiar with the individual securities owned by your target mutual fund. Make sure you're comfortable with the fund's investment priorities.

Also, read up on the credentials and track record of the fund's manager. The fund may boast a great 10-year performance record, but if the manager has just signed on, that track record may not be meaningful.

Understanding economics

They call economics "the dreary science," which is an overstatement, perhaps. But remember: Investing is neither sexy nor emotional. It's a financial-growth tool based on solid data, so a little understanding of economics can help.

In some cases, general economic conditions can affect performance in certain business sectors. Understanding these relationships can help you in two ways. First, it will help you manage your portfolio by providing guidance on the timing issues surrounding investing. (We are not suggesting market timing as an investment strategy. However, even if your investment perspective is long term, an understanding of economics can provide insight. For example, knowing that consumer stocks don't fair well when interest rates are rising can help you in your investments or dispositions.) Second, understanding how the broader economy can affect investments can tell you why your investments are faring well or poorly. You'll have an explanation rooted in data, so you'll be less likely to make emotion-based decisions.

Here are some aspects of economics to keep in mind:

Interest rates

Interest rates have a significant impact on investment markets and the overall economy. If you appreciate the cyclical nature of interest rates, you won't overreact to what appear to be sudden and inexplicable changes in the markets.

Business cycles

Inflation and recession are two common business cycles. Investment sectors tend to exhibit characteristic behavior during these cycles. When you understand cycle-related behavior, you'll avoid emotion-based decisions.

Leading and lagging economic indicators

Economists read dozens of indicators for clues as to where the economy is going. "Leading indicators" relate to the future of the economy; "lagging indicators" tell us where the economy has been. New building permits, for example, are a leading indicator, helping us predict the immediate future in the construction industry and perhaps consumer confidence in the economy. On the other hand, the change in the consumer price index for services is a lagging indicator.

Does this mean you should run out and invest in the stocks of building contractors if the number of new building permits soars? Hardly. As with interest rates and business cycles, understanding indicators broadens and deepens your appreciation of the forces at work in the markets, making you a more rational investor.

Understanding tax and estate law

Ultimately, the most important outcome for your portfolio is its after-tax return—that is, what goes into your pocket. Yet many fund managers quote their performance on a pretax basis. Don't be confused here. If your financial blueprint calls for a 10-percent return on investment, make sure you're getting that 10 percent after taxes.

Different investment vehicles generate different tax consequences. Mutual funds, for example, may pay capital gains distributions to you, even in years when the fund's value doesn't grow. This is the worst of both worlds: losing money in your portfolio and paying taxes on top of it. If you research the practices of target funds, you can avoid this unappetizing situation.

Consider also what happens to your portfolio upon your death. Tax and estate law determine the financial consequences for your heirs, yet these laws change frequently. Therefore, you must structure your investment portfolio so that it can accommodate tax and estate law modifications. For portfolio management purposes, factor in the following:

Your tax bracket

Now that you're married, your combined income may be significantly greater than each of you achieved individually. As a result, your maximum tax bracket may increase, making it more difficult to achieve the after-tax performance you've outlined in your financial game plan.

Tax-advantaged investments

You want to exploit these for all they're worth, yet that means keeping up with changes in the underlying laws. Over the past 30 years, one could have made a nifty career by charting and advising on the changes in IRA regulations alone. Keep current to keep ahead.

Estate taxes

When planning to provide for your heirs, always consider the net impact of estate and transfer taxes. Let's suppose, for example, that the majority of your portfolio is in 401(k) and IRA accounts. When you bequeath these, your heirs must satisfy traditional estate and inheritance taxes, but they also could be responsible for income taxes, because those were deferred during your lifetime as the accounts were appreciating. Without appropriate tax planning, the value of your estate can be vastly reduced by the tax burden on your heirs. (We'll discuss estate planning in greater detail in Chapter 12.)

Options for managing your portfolio

Some people are excited by the prospect of managing their portfolios; they feel knowledgeable and confident, and they like taking charge of their financial future. For others, particularly those with a limited financial background, the challenge of portfolio management can be intimidating. Wherever you fall in this continuum, there are options available:

Option 1—Do it yourself.

Proper portfolio management requires money and time. Oddly, the Internet has been both a boon and a curse in this area. It offers promising new tools, such as data-rich Web sites and financial calculators, that appear to make the job easy. Information, however, is not the same as knowledge. Information does not give you perspective. Research reports and financial calculators are great if you understand the underlying assumptions. If you don't, they could be vehicles to financial folly.

There are no shortcuts here. If you want to manage your money on your own, you'll need to invest a great deal of time educating yourself, then even more time to monitor and modify your investments. And if, after all your study, you find yourself making mistakes, think about the marital conflict you could be inviting.

Most people find that their time is better spent advancing their careers than managing their portfolios. Even after absorbing the fees of a professional manager, you'll likely be better off. That time you dedicate to your career will yield more investment-ready income, and you'll avoid the mistakes and marital dissension that often are the by-products of portfolio self-management.

Option 2—Take advice from friends and family.

Don't do it. Period.

When you marry, you'll find yourselves awash in well-wishers with advice about what to do with your money. But each of these would-be advisors has a different agenda, different goals, and a different level of risk tolerance. What works for your cousin may not work for you. And if the informal advice leads to investments that turn sour, it can damage familial relationships and create tension and resentment in your marriage.

Typically, a friend or relation bragging about a killing in the market isn't telling you the whole story. When was the last time your brother-in-law burst into the room and exclaimed, "I just lost a fortune on Anapanaconda, and I wanted you to be the first to know." Doesn't happen, does it?

Option 3—Seek out a professional.

Hiring a professional advisor typically will provide you with the best opportunity to achieve your financial goals. This assumes, of course, that your advisor is credible and knowledgeable. Not all are. The last few decades have brought explosive growth in the number of people who call themselves financial advisors.

Approach this task as you would the assignment of engaging a new doctor or dentist. Interview a number of prospects to gauge their skills and background and to establish a comfort level for you. Inquire about their:

Credentials

Is your potential advisor a Certified Financial Planner (CFP)? CFPs are educated in all areas of financial planning and typically provide the most well-rounded advice. If your candidate is a CFP, that's a strong plus.

Fee structure

Financial planners can be compensated in a variety of ways. Commissions, flat fees, hourly fees, and fees based on a percentage of assets are common structures. There are advantages and disadvantages to each. If your planner works on a commission basis, for example, your charge will be based on the number and size of transactions implemented. That's fair enough, but if your planner recommends transactions that generate commissions without enhancing your long-term prospects, you haven't saved anything and may be losing quite a bit.

For their part, hourly fees can make you reluctant to communicate with your advisor, knowing that you're paying out of pocket each time you pick up the phone.

If your fee is based on a percentage of the assets in your portfolio, you gain several advantages. First, your advisor has a stake in your success; as the value of your portfolio increases, so, too, do the management fees. In addition, you can be comfortable knowing that your advisor will not churn out transactions just to generate commissions.

With fee structures, there is no right or wrong approach. The best fee structure is the one that maximizes your flexibility and the value of your relationship with your advisor.

Investment philosophy

You must be comfortable with the basic philosophy of your advisor. Does your advisor try to time the market or favor a long-term, asset-allocation approach? How will your advisor respond to market declines? What mistakes has your advisor made in the past? Probe all of these areas.

Other clients

Most prospects will provide you with the names of current customers; inevitably, those customers will offer glowing reviews of the advisors. There is a self-serving aspect to customer referrals, but it still makes sense to use them. You can gain some understanding of the advisor's services and approach from an existing client.

Review procedures

How will your financial plan be reviewed? Your circumstances will change; your portfolio must change as well. Regular meetings with your financial advisor are essential to review performance and initiate changes. Determine up front if your candidate returns phone calls promptly, has the support staff to monitor your portfolio and initiate contacts with you, and is amenable to meetings with you.

Finally, even as you interview candidates, make sure that they're interviewing you as well. Your prospective advisor should be trying to learn about who you are, your financial goals, and, your risk tolerance. After all, professional advisors need to establish a comfort level as well. If there aren't any questions coming your way, you may want to move along to the next candidate.

 *Pillow talk*

How can you find a professional financial advisor? Word of mouth may be the best way. Even though you don't want to rely on family and friends for investment advice, they can lead you to an advisor they trust.

Once you accumulate a certain level of assets, you'll also find yourself the target of some strange phone calls. These mystery callers are financial advisors trying to sell you their services. We've never figured out exactly how they get names. Perhaps they bought subscriber lists from magazines or Internet services. In any case, we've always found it odd that people whom we've never met will ask us to entrust to them our entire fortunes, such as they are. We can't warm up to cold calls from financial advisors.

However you identify candidates to help manage your money, you should interview your prospects as a couple and work together to draft a list of questions. Here are some to get you started:

- $ Are you a Certified Financial Planner? Do you have other special skills that are certified and relevant?
- $ What are your fees, and how are they structured?
- $ What type of support staff do you have?
- $ How often will we communicate, and will we do so by phone, e-mail, or some other means?
- $ Will we be dealing with you directly? If not, which staff member will handle our account?
- $ How often will we review our portfolio with you?
- $ In general, how would you describe your investment philosophy?
- $ What has been your greatest success as a financial advisor?
- $ What has been your biggest mistake as a financial advisor?
- $ Can you give us the names of any current customers who could discuss your capabilities and services?

Chapter 9

Planning Your Taxes
So They Won't Be Deathly

lanning your life together is a process full of unexpected delights and wonder, an adventure that you
could only imagine as a single person. Then you
open the mail one day to find your 1040 form,
and it's as if the S.S. *Marriage* has run aground, your
marvelous journey broken up on the rocky shoals of income tax.

There's no way around it. Taxes are a significant and unavoidable expense. For most of us, the pain seldom is soothed by looking around at all the benefits—public transportation, well-maintained
highways, school systems, trash collection, protection from hostile
nations—that our taxes bring us. Death and taxes may be certain,
but the amount of taxes you pay can be modified by savvy planning. A proactive approach to your taxes is essential. Too often,
couples approach their tax responsibilities with a feeling of help-
lessness; it's the law and there's nothing you can do. If you're a slave
to this mentality, you may overlook tax plan-
ning and all the benefits it can bring.

The bottom line to tax planning is
to reduce this expense to its lowest
possible number and, we might add,

to do so completely within all applicable laws. Tax considerations affect every aspect of your financial planning, from budgeting to goal-setting, and on through to investing.

For example, when you project the amount you need to save each month to accomplish your financial goals, your projections are based in part on the "after-tax" rates of return for your investments. If you don't factor taxes into your calculations, you may come up way short. Let's say you're planning on a 12-percent return on investments over a 20-year period, but your after-tax rate of return is only 10 percent. That's a difference of 40 percent—a major hit, and that doesn't include the compounding effect over time.

Choosing the investment vehicles that are most suitable for you depends on a proper understanding of your income tax bracket, responsibilities, and opportunities. You won't know whether to invest in tax-free or tax-deferred investment vehicles if you don't know the particular tax implications for you.

Thus, tax considerations roll through your financial planning. And marriage brings many possible changes. Filing status, withholding from your income, deductions, eligibility for retirement plans—all these factors, and the related tax consequences, now may be different.

This chapter is designed to help you understand a broad range of tax issues and apply this knowledge to your financial planning, so that you won't be leaving money on the table. Efficiency with your income taxes will allow you to maximize your overall financial situation.

Withholding

Withholding is the amount withheld from your paycheck by your employer and sent directly to the Internal Revenue Service. (If you're self-employed, you handle your own withholding via quarterly estimated tax payments.) In effect, the federal government gathers taxes from you every pay period, rather than having to collect the entire amount from you annually. It works for the government, and it can work well for you as well. Many people find it easier to live without the small amount withheld from each paycheck than to produce an onerous tax payment each April 15.

The amount withheld is based in part upon the allowances you claimed on the W-4 form you completed when you were hired. Now that you're married, you may want to reevaluate your allowance claims and the corresponding amount of salary withheld; the more allowances you claim, the less the withholding. This may seem a smallish area to be concerned about in the overall picture of financial planning, because it all comes out in the wash; your tax bill doesn't change whether you pay in one lump sump or through 26 or 52 small pieces of your salary. But there are some fairly important reasons to assure that your withholding is aligned with your income tax liability.

First, if you overestimate your tax obligation and have too much salary withheld, you're not utilizing your money wisely. Some folks prefer to maximize their withholding because it denies them access to money they would otherwise spend, and it helps provide a tax refund every year. But consider the downside. The IRS doesn't pay interest on overpayments. You could be investing the money you're overpaying in taxes. If you're maximizing withholding as a way of imposing discipline on yourself, try this approach instead: Reduce your withholding and earmark the difference for automatic contributions to your 401(k) or other pension plan.

On the other hand, if you're not withholding enough, it could leave you with a substantial federal tax obligation, a financial penalty from the IRS for insufficient payments, or both. Penalties always are a useless expense.

To get it right, invest some time to understand your tax situation, and don't wait until you file your first income tax return as a couple. Withholding is affecting your finances right now and requires immediate attention. For help, check out IRS publication 919 entitled *Is My Withholding Correct?* You can call the IRS at (800) 829-1040 to order the publication or view it on-line *(www.irs.gov/ forms_pubs/pubs.html)*. The publication includes W-4 worksheets to help you calculate a withholding level that's appropriate for you.

Filing status

Your tax rates are determined in part by your filing status. This never was an issue when you were single, as there were no choices. As a couple, however, you have the option to file as "married filing jointly" or "married filing separately." Your overall income tax bill likely will increase or decrease based on your filing status and income level, but the choice of filing status is not clear-cut.

Let's look at several hypothetical situations and how they could affect the filing status decision. In our first example, where one spouse is employed and the other is not, and the couple files jointly, chances are their tax rates will decline due to increased exemptions and a more generous upper-end limit within the tax bracket. So far, so good.

Now consider another example, where both couples continue to work after marriage. Because income limitations for all tax rates are less than double for married couples than they are for single filers, this hypothetical couple may land in a higher tax bracket than each experienced before marriage if they file jointly. This phenomenon, by the way, is the infamous "marriage penalty." Congress has begun to recognize the problems with the marriage penalty and, through The Economic Growth and Tax Reconciliation Act of 2001, is phasing in some changes over the years 2005–2009.

There are other factors in the filing-status decision as well. Tax rates for separate filers are one-half the joint rates, so filing separately doesn't provide a break in the gross percentages. Filing separately can enable you to maximize certain categories of deduction; at the same time, separate filing may limit your opportunity to fully utilize other potential advantages, including certain tax credits, education benefits, taxes on Social Security benefits, IRA eligibility, limits on taking capital losses, exclusion on the sale of a home, and rental real-estate deductions. If you live in a community property state and plan on "married filing separately" status, be sure to check with your state for a clear understanding of your ability to separate income, exemptions, and deductions.

Clearly, there's much to consider in the area of filing status. Let's throw one more variable into the mix. If you file a joint return, each of you must sign it, and each of you is responsible for it in its entirety. Should one spouse fail to report income or otherwise play fast and loose with the rules, both spouses are equally responsible for the misdeed. Thus, your willingness to file a joint return, quite apart from the many financial issues involved, depends on the mutual trust you've developed. If either of you harbors any doubts about the completeness or veracity of your return, you may be better off filing separately. It's not terrific testimony to the solidity of your marriage, but it can keep a law-abiding partner free of liability.

Personal and dependent exemptions

A certain portion of your income will be exempt from income tax, with the exemption based on the number of people in your household—you, your spouse, and any dependent children.

The key here is to understand the criteria to ensure you're taking full advantage of your exemptions. For example, you may be supporting children from a previous marriage; these children may qualify as exemptions. Are you supporting aging parents, a phenomenon that has grown as Baby Boomers have achieved middle age? Your dependent parents may qualify as exemptions as well. Explore all the options here, as exemptions represent free money.

Because exemptions carry a "phase-out" feature, your filing status can affect your ability to claim them. As a single tax filer, your income may never have reached the phase-out trigger. With your combined income as a couple, you may well hit the income ceiling (the phase-out amounts for joint filers begin at less than double that of single filers) and find that your exemptions are limited. This means more taxes, a clear disadvantage of joint filing.

Itemized deductions or standard deductions?

As a single filer, you may have opted for the standard deduction, the flat amount the IRS allows you to deduct from your taxable income in light of various expenses. If you're filing a joint return, you may find that itemizing your deductions will save you money. This happens if the total of your itemized deductions would exceed the standard deduction.

If you own a home, for example, the interest payments on your mortgage or home-improvement loan are a deduction you can itemize. Other qualifying deductions that can be itemized include state and local taxes, charitable contributions, and medical and dental costs (after a certain threshold is reached). Although they may require more documentation, you also can itemize expenses for an office in your home, education costs, casualty and theft losses, and certain business expenses, including meals, travel, entertainment, and automobile maintenance.

As with personal and dependent exemptions, phase-out rules apply to itemized deductions, and there is no phase-out relief for joint filers.

To determine if itemizing is an advantage for you, you'll need to compute a tentative total of itemized deductions and compare it to the standard deduction. If you do opt for itemizing, remember to document all the expenses you're itemizing. The IRS may look askance at that trip to Las Vegas you're itemizing as a business expense unless you can support it with appropriate documentation.

Taxes and your investments

A key part of managing your income taxes is managing your income. What we mean by this is that as your income increases, it could land you in a higher tax bracket, forcing you to yield an ever-increasing percentage of your income in taxes. Over time, the impact of those lost dollars, and the compounding those dollars could have generated, can be quite significant. If you understand tax-advantaged investments, though, you can fully utilize these to minimize the tax bite. There are two broad categories of tax-advantaged investments: tax-free and tax-deferred. Let's take a look at each.

Tax-free investments

With these vehicles, any income generated by the investment is exempt from federal income taxes. You never have to pay income taxes on your earnings from tax-free investments. There is a catch: Most tax-free vehicles require investment on an after-tax basis, meaning that you've already paid income taxes on the money used to make the investment.

Tax-deferred investments

As the name suggests, taxes on any income generated by these vehicles are deferred until some point in the future. Many categories of tax-deferred investments, including 401(k) plans and traditional IRAs, allow for investment with before-tax dollars, which is a considerable up-front benefit. However, all distributions from such accounts are subject to federal income taxes, because none of that money has been taxed to that point.

Types of income and tax rates

As you consider the tax consequences of investment vehicles, it's important to remember that not all income is taxed equally. The tax code establishes several categories of income, along with corresponding tax rates. The major categories are:

Ordinary income

Most income falls into this category. Ordinary income is taxed at the applicable percentage, according to IRS tax tables.

Interest and dividend income

No matter its source, interest and dividend income is considered ordinary income and taxed accordingly.

Capital gains

Capital gains (and losses, for that matter), are generated when you acquire, and later sell, an investment. Buy stocks for $100,000, sell them for $200,000, and you have a capital gain of $100,000. How this gain is taxed depends on how long you've held the asset. If you've owned it for less than one year, the capital gain is considered "short-term" and taxed as ordinary income. If you've owned it for more than one year, the appreciation is considered a "long-term" capital gain and taxed at a lower rate. If you own an investment for more than five years, an even lower capital gains tax is applied, provided the investment was acquired after the year 2000.

•••

Now we're set to review some specific investments and their tax consequences

401(k) plans

If you set out to create the perfect investment vehicle, you'd whip up one that would be widely available through employers.

It would offer benefits now and benefits later. And employers would swirl a little icing on the cake by making contributions for their workers.

Great news: You don't have to invent this Vegematic of investments. It already exists, and it's called 401(k). Many employers offer these retirement plans—the number has expanded exponentially in recent years—and they're available to the self-employed as well.

Although some companies allow for after-tax contributions to 401(k) plans, contributions typically are made with pretax dollars, so there are no taxes now on the money you contribute. Your contributions, which otherwise would go to the government as taxes, enjoy a compounding effect over time, a tremendous benefit to you. Throw in the employer "match" and you have a gift that keeps on giving.

Alas, even this "perfect" investment vehicle has its limitations. For one, any withdrawals prior to age 59 1/2 are taxed; in most cases, the IRS imposes a penalty of 10 percent as well. Also, when you reach age 70 1/2, you must begin taking distributions from your account, based on your life expectancy. You'll want to factor mandatory distributions into your overall retirement planning.

These few regulations notwithstanding, 401(k) plans are an amazing tax-planning opportunity. Don't limit your contributions to the amount your company will match. Max this baby out. If you fully exploit your 401(k) plan or plans, you may be able to offset the impact of the higher tax bracket your marriage may have brought.

Individual Retirement Accounts (IRAs)

The popularity of Individual Retirement Accounts (IRAs) has grown so substantially that the federal government has created several variations to fit different circumstances and needs. Although the fundamental principles of each variant are about the same, there are some key differences.

Traditional IRAs

With traditional IRAs, your contributions provide you with a tax deduction equal to the amount of your contribution; in effect, your contribution gains pretax status. The money in your account grows tax-deferred, making it quite a useful tool.

There are limitations. Participation is restricted if you exceed certain income limitations and qualify for an employer-sponsored plan. Your maximum contribution is capped and at a lower level than that of many employer-sponsored plans. As with 401(k) plans, withdrawals prior to age 59 1/2 are taxed and assessed a 10-percent penalty, although there are certain exceptions. Mandatory distributions begin at age 70 1/2.

Roth IRAs

The most important distinguishing feature of Roth IRAs is that your contributions are made with after-tax dollars, but your account grows tax-free. As a result, the long-term benefits are great.

Eligibility requirements for Roth IRAs are somewhat more liberal than those for traditional IRAs. You also have the ability to access your account without penalty if your money has been invested for at least five years and you're spending the distributions for qualified purposes. These include higher education, medical expenses, and health-insurance premiums for certain unemployed participants.

Nondeductible IRAs

If you're not eligible for a traditional IRA or a Roth IRA, you still can take advantage of this vehicle through a non-deductible IRA. It's the same in most regards as a traditional IRA, except that you don't get a deduction for your current taxes. You're making contributions with after-tax dollars, but your earnings are tax-deferred. The benefits still are great.

Tax-free municipal bonds vs. taxable bonds

Tax-free municipal bonds are a popular and straightforward source of income. As the name suggests, this income is tax-free, but there is an important caveat: Tax-free municipals offer a lower rate of return than taxable bonds. Which is the best option for you? In our Pillow Talk section on page 141, you'll find a quick and easy formula that you can apply as a couple to determine which type of bonds works better for you.

Capital gains and losses

Capital gains generate taxes, but you can offset your gains with capital losses. Losing money is never a cause for celebration, but it does provide you with the opportunity to ease your tax burden. Many couples wait until the end of the year to identify eligible capital losses, but there is one situation where waiting may not pay off: the phenomenon known as "wash sales."

Under the rules for wash sales, if you sell a security and want to declare a loss associated with that holding, you must wait 30 days before buying back that particular security. If you don't mind being out of that investment for at least 30 days, wash rules are no big deal. Still, they do represent a reason for year-round consideration of potential capital losses, rather than a rushed December sale that could keep you out of a stock for 30 days.

Personally held mutual funds

We like mutual funds as a tool for diversification of your investments, but they can present interesting tax issues. Mutual funds are required to pass through their income and capital gains to shareholders on an annual basis. With individual securities, you as the investor determine when to take gains. Mutual funds buy and sell stocks and bonds without any input from you, giving you no control over capital gains distributions from year to year.

This can be a troubling and unpredictable variable in your tax planning, and it doesn't necessarily matter if your fund did not perform well in a given year. During the year, the fund may have sold securities that had appreciated significantly. That generates capital gains and corresponding taxes for you, even though you may not have been on board to enjoy the full measure of the gains.

The remedy here is to research the potential for capital gains built up in any fund you target. Check with the fund's managers. Ask them to estimate their potential capital gains distributions for the year. In today's competitive investment environment, you may find that it's worth leaving your current fund and making a lateral move to another fund that matches your investment objectives but isn't expecting a hefty capital gains distribution.

In addition, explore the "turnover" of any fund you target. Does the manager trade frequently, activity that can generate more potential gains? Is it a newer fund, with very little build-up in capital gains? Is it an "index" fund, with trading activity tied to a particular financial index, thus limiting sales and capital gains?

These are the questions to ask as you consider switching funds. Remember, however, that switching works only if you haven't built up sizable capital gains in your current fund. If you switch in that situation, you'll get hit with the full measure of the capital gains from the sale of the fund.

Annuities

Offered by insurance companies, annuities are an investment vehicle that provides tax-deferred growth. You buy annuities with after-tax dollars, so there's no immediate tax benefit.

Annuities can offer a fixed rate or variable rates of return; variable annuities feature a variety of subaccounts, typically mutual funds. Because annuity income growth is tax-deferred, it may seem an obvious selection over direct participation in mutual funds, where taxes are not deferred. But there are some subtle issues here.

First, you'll experience additional expenses associated with purchasing a mutual fund within an annuity. You'll end up paying more than you would if you purchased the mutual fund directly. In addition, the IRS imposes a 10-percent penalty for withdrawals prior to age 59.

Other issues include the taxation of earnings when withdrawn and the loss of a stepped-up cost basis at death. You also could incur a surrender charge assessed by the insurance company if withdrawals exceed a specified amount and occur within a certain period of time.

On the plus side, annuities sometimes offer positive features, such as death benefits. In recent years, annuities have come a long way in reducing expenses and offering more flexibility. A general rule of thumb on annuities is this: The higher your tax bracket, the more likely you are to benefit from annuities because of the tax-deferred status of your gains. The best advice is to thoroughly explore internal expenses and surrender fees before jumping in.

Professional advice

Annuities are complex, but no more vexing than many other aspects of the tax code. We've covered some important facets of the code and how they may affect your tax planning, but there are other issues to consider. This is one area of financial planning where professional advice may be a must. You may not want a consultant to make your investment decisions for you, but you should ask your tax professional to outline the options and consequences for the investments you propose to make as a couple.

Pillow talk

Nobody has ever suggested that a lively discussion of municipal bonds will add spice to your marriage, but there is a simple and fun way to determine whether you should be in taxable bonds or tax-free municipal bonds. Get out your pencils and paper and work through this calculation:

$ **Step 1**—Begin with the number "1." Easy enough.

$ **Step 2**—Subtract from 1 your income tax rate. If you're in the 28 percent bracket, subtract .28 from 1 for an answer of .72.

$ **Step 3**—Divide the projected rate of return on your tax-free bond by the answer you got in Step 2. For example, if you're targeting a municipal bond earning 4 percent tax-free, divide 4 percent by .72 for an answer of 5.56 percent.

This answer, 5.56 percent, represents what a taxable bond would have to pay to provide you with the same end result as a tax-free municipal bond. If you can do better than 5.56 percent with a taxable bond, this calculation tells you that you're better off, even though you'll pay taxes on the income. If you can't beat 5.56 percent with a taxable bond, stick with the tax-free vehicle.

Profile

Paige and Michael Rafferty: From Condo Magic to Dream Home—and a Few Trade-offs

With a degree in financial planning, Paige worked first for a financial advisory firm. Her current employer is a New York-based mutual fund, for which she sells and markets throughout the mid-Atlantic region. Michael worked for a decade in cardiology equipment sales and now is in an equally important and timely field: selling software tools that help pharmaceutical companies expedite the drug-approval process.

In the late 1990s when Paige's career necessitated relocation, she found and rented a Maryland condo in greater Washington. Who should be living in the condo below but Michael. Their acquaintanceship blossomed into romance and, in 1999, marriage. Paige was 27 and Michael 32 when they wed.

Although the annals of marriage may be replete with the fortuitous, magical meetings such as that of Paige and Michael, this couple has determined that their financial future will be anything but accidental.

$ 142 $

Communication

Paige is a detail-oriented planner. Michael, although no less meticulous, may be a bit more relaxed. The couple discovered early on that, due to these initial differences in approach, regular communication would be essential in helping them achieve both marital harmony and financial security.

"I wouldn't say there's a structure, but we definitely have free-flowing communications," Paige says. "The channels are always open."

"I'm absolutely the one who wants to stimulate the economy more. Michael will say, 'Do we need this?' If I can convince him that we do, then I've done my job, too."

Regular communications also have revealed differences in investment philosophy—and ways to bridge the gap.

"Paige was pretty structured with investing in mutual funds," Michael recalls. "I love playing the stock market. I've made some great picks and some poor ones. Paige hasn't hesitated to point out the poor ones to me. I'm a little more conservative now. That's one thing I've compromised on."

Asset consolidation

With a number of years in the workforce behind them, Paige and Michael each brought assets to the marriage; consolidation wasn't a major concern, because most of those assets were earmarked for their marriage ceremony and home purchase.

"Our parents chipped in for the marriage," Paige says, "but we wanted them to save their money for their own retirement."

Nevertheless, there were life insurance policies, IRAs, mutual funds, and 401(k) plans to consider. Michael developed a filing system (one labeled folder for each account) to ensure that the beneficiary was changed for each asset.

"It was a time-consuming process," Paige recalls. "I even forgot an account for which we wanted to change the beneficiary."

Ultimately, they were more than satisfied with their approach to asset consolidation.

"There was no need for a prenuptial agreement," Michael says. "There were no issues."

Trade-offs

Perhaps the fundamental decision that Paige and Michael made early in their marriage was to purchase a home, a 4,100-square-foot beauty in North Potomac that's as close to a dream house as most newlyweds can afford.

"Around here real estate appreciates well," Paige says. "We knew if we put it off for a year or two, we would lose the opportunity to live where we do."

Would they be able to acquire the home and have sufficient income left for other needs? They answered the question with the help of some joint discussion and planning.

"It was pretty nerve-wracking at first," Michael says, "but we worked the numbers out on paper and saw that we could do it."

A big chunk of their income would need to be reserved for the down payment and monthly mortgage payments, and there would be other trade-offs as well. Says Paige: "We knew we would have to accumulate furniture slowly, and that we wouldn't be able to bank as much because of the bigger mortgage. We try to eat at home more. Sure, you may splurge on the weekend, but that's one area we try to control. We knew there would be trade-offs, but we view the house as an investment for the long term."

Checking accounts, credit cards, and budgeting

Paige and Michael were accustomed to living independently; each also encounters business expenses that ultimately will be reimbursed but which frequently need immediate attention. To preserve a measure of independence and maintain maximum flexibility for those business expenses, they became a three checking-account family: one joint account and two individual accounts. Each also has a credit card in one partner's name only.

"We pay all household expenses from the joint account," Paige says. "We look at what we owe, and based on that, we each put money into the joint account."

They operate without a formal budget, but they review fixed and variable expenses each month and plan their spending accordingly. They've grown quite comfortable with this arrangement that allows them to preserve some independence as they pursue common goals.

"We know we each have our own expenses, and we know there's no abuse," Paige says. "We have respect for each other. We still practice 'Pay yourself first' and invest automatically each month."

Investments and long-term goals

Children are definitely in their future, so they've begun to incorporate family considerations into their planning. For one thing, Paige intends to keep working even as she and Michael raise their children.

"I feel a strong sense of identity that I gain from having a career," she says. "I don't want to lose sight of that. Everyone will benefit from my continuing to work—my husband, my kids, and me. I am hoping to achieve a sense of balance with family, home, and career."

Although their regular discussions have made Michael a more prudent investor, they've also introduced Paige to the growth potential of the stock market. In fact, she's opened her own account, although she continues to believe in professional money management.

"Everything I do is long-term," she reports. "I'm in an accumulation mode. When we get to a certain level, we will have professional portfolio management. I prefer mutual funds, where you're diversified among 50 to 60 stocks, rather than riding on one or two stocks. We plan to diversify among different managers as well."

Professional advice

They're a few years away from needing professional portfolio management, but they have engaged an expert, a former colleague of Michael, to advise them on insurance coverage.

"We shopped around to make sure we purchased adequate life insurance and disability insurance," Paige says.

Advice for newlyweds

$ **Paige:** "You really have to outline who's going to handle what. Figure out your goals and a time frame, even though you know that very little will work as planned and you will need to make changes. Be flexible but realistic. Learn to 'pay yourself first.' If you develop that discipline, it will help in the long run."

$ **Michael:** "For young people, it's easy to get in debt over your head. My advice is to maintain a simple philosophy: Don't spend what you don't have. If you have to go into debt, make sure it's not long-term debt."

Chapter 10

Keeping Good Records: Write It, Copy It, File It, Review It

As citizens of the 21st century, we like to believe that we are striding confidently to a paperless society, where all our important transactions are handled by computers that we can access from anywhere. All that may happen someday, but for now, think of how vitally important paper documents remain to your marriage.

If you buy a house, the deed is your proof of ownership. Claim deductions on your income taxes and the IRS may ask you to document those with paper receipts. Need to determine if a physician you'd like to visit is in your HMO's network? Fair enough. But first you must page through that thick provider list—more paper—to make sure your doctor is a participant.

It's clear that paper documents continue to play a critical role in financial planning. And now that you're married, you'll have more than double the paperwork to consider. You may be tempted to deal with it in one fell swoop—with a shredder. A better approach to documentation is to jointly discuss your

$ 147 $

needs and develop a plan for saving and storage. Why is this important? That's what this chapter is about.

When you communicate as a couple about your documents, each of you gains a better understanding of your spouse's important issues. This awareness will help you create a strong foundation for your financial planning. Discussing documents will enable you to identify any gaps in your financial game plan and lead you to remedial action.

As you become comfortable with your document filing system, you'll find it a valuable resource for monitoring your financial situation. Think, for example, of your investment statements. If you toss those aside once you've read them, you may not remember the information exactly. But if you file those statements, you can pull them out at any time and know precisely how your investments are performing. To our way of thinking, filing and monitoring are companion aspects of financial planning.

You can begin these dual processes by identifying an appropriate location for document storage. Some couples use a safe deposit box at a financial institution. This certainly maximizes security, but most boxes aren't capacious enough to store everything you need. Even beyond that, if you have to run to the bank each time you want to save a receipt, how likely are you to do that?

Our preference is for a repository that's both safe and accessible. A fireproof filing cabinet in your home will do the job nicely. Now you're ready to discuss, gather, and store these documents:

Marriage license

When you change the status or beneficiary of your accounts or policies, you may be required to provide proof of marriage. You may encounter other situations as well where documenting your marriage facilitates matters. So it's a good idea to make copies of your marriage license for attachment to submissions as necessary and to preserve and store the original.

Social Security numbers

If you're like us, you can remember your own Social Security number but would be hard-pressed to recite your spouse's. These days, however, it's not uncommon to be asked for both partners' numbers; this is particularly true of Internet transactions, where Social Security numbers are a popular means of secure identification. Quite apart from the Net, you almost certainly will be asked your spouse's Social Security number when submitting medical or dental reimbursement claims.

For all these reasons, make sure that you and your spouse exchange Social Security numbers and that each of your numbers is stored in your filing cabinet.

Health insurance documents

Keep all your health insurance documents in your filing cabinet. If we had a dollar for every time our medical insurer asked us to refile a claim, which of course we then had to scramble to find, we'd be rich and retired. You can do a better job by saving and filing everything.

If you and your spouse are covered under separate policies, make sure you exchange health-insurance information and discuss the procedures, including notification and referral forms, of each insurer. This mutual understanding can become critical if one of you needs medical assistance but is unable to provide the information the insurer requires.

Automobile-related documents

Exchange driver's license numbers. You might never be called on to provide your spouse's operator number, but unusual circumstances can arise, and it never hurts to be prepared.

Copy your insurance and owner's cards; keep one set in each car, and store one set in your filing cabinet. Some motorists keep these cards in the glove compartment only. That gives you ready access, but if your car is stolen, you'll need to replace the cards.

Employee benefits statements

This information helps give you a handle on your benefits, a key component of your overall financial plan. Just as important, your spouse will have quick access to your benefits history and availability if something happens to you.

Investment statements

Create a file for each investment account, including IRAs and 401(k) plans. This is extremely important for tracking income tax-related issues, especially the cost basis for each of your investments. If you're contributing to a mutual fund or purchasing individual stocks each pay period, there's no way you'll remember each purchase price and no way you can accurately compute capital gains or losses upon the sale of the assets without comprehensive records.

Insurance documents

Keep a separate file for every insurance policy. Life insurance, disability insurance, auto insurance, appliance insurance: Each policy gets a separate file. In addition to the original policy, maintain a history of your premium payments and any changes you've made to the policy, such as a new beneficiary designation. If a policy is set to expire, you'll have a great tool for reviewing your premium payments and deciding if a little price shopping is in order.

Although warranties on appliances may not be as important as insurance policies, we recommend you preserve those as well. Perhaps one file for all warranties will suffice, rather than a separate file for each warranty. When that VCR breaks down, you won't know if you're entitled to free repair unless you've saved the warranty in a convenient place.

Income tax documents

Consider several categories of information here. First would be records of any expenses that you plan to itemize as deductions: charitable contributions, retirement plan contributions, state and local tax records, and receipts for business expenses. This latter category can be expansive, covering everything from receipts for business-related meals to highway toll receipts (if those trips were related to your business).

The best practice here is to begin a new file each calendar year for deduction documentation. The more organized you are in this matter throughout the year, the easier it will be for you and your accountant to prepare your income tax return and for you to provide any documentation that the IRS requests.

The second category of documents to be preserved are your tax returns themselves, including federal, state, and local returns. Under federal law, the IRS has the right to audit your return for up to three years without citing any reason. If a back tax obligation is suspected, the time limit for audits is six years. For suspected fraud or failure to file, there is no time limit on audits.

However, we don't recommend that you automatically pitch your returns after six years. Your income tax return includes investment-related information, such as dividend and capital gains distributions you received. Thus, it makes sense to preserve any tax return for as long as you hold investments that have been reported on that tax return.

Home purchase and maintenance documents

If you've purchased a home, keep a file that includes your mortgage information and receipts for any expenses related to the upkeep of your residence. When you sell your house, some home-maintenance expenses can be included in your cost basis, lowering your capital gain and subsequent tax obligation. If you don't document these expenses and preserve the receipts, chances are you'll forget some of them. (It's a good idea to explore the exclusions for home sale gains along with corresponding guidelines. These issues are particularly important if each spouse brings a residence to the marriage.)

Review this file regularly so that you're always aware of the interest rate on your mortgage, your mortgage balance, expenses such as property taxes that are rolled into your mortgage payments, and when your mortgage will be paid off. Your awareness of these issues will help you maximize your dollars and efficiently prepare for retirement. For example, if you know that your mortgage payments of $1,000 include $200 each month for property taxes and homeowners' insurance, you'll also know that your expenses will be $800 less, not $1,000 less, when the mortgage is paid off.

Monthly income and expenses

Saving your pay stubs admittedly is not the highest priority of your documentation plan. Nevertheless, we recommend that you incorporate this practice. You may need to produce evidence of your income if you apply for a loan, and saving the stubs will help you identify any errors in your pay. Because pay stubs are cumulative, we suggest that you maintain the most recent stub.

As for such regular expenses as utilities, you need to preserve this information so that you can evaluate your current budget and make any necessary modifications. You can record these expenses manually or with a computer software program, such as Quicken or Microsoft Money. Once you've recorded these expenses, whether or not you preserve the stubs is a matter of your preference. If you intend to deduct utility and similar costs as home-office expenses, hang on to the paperwork as backup.

Record-keeping and your budget

Creating and sticking to a monthly budget is one of the most critical tasks in achieving financial security. Consistent performance in this area will be a key factor in your ability to avoid debt and save for your long-term goals. If you're constantly dealing with unforeseen expenses or increases in costs for your budgeted items, you'll be playing catch-up instead of proactively achieving financial success.

Tracking your monthly income and expenses will help you understand the impact of cost changes and gain the upper hand. As certain costs fluctuate, you'll be well positioned to make adjustments elsewhere. Let's suppose, for example, that rising energy prices cause sharp increases in your monthly utilities costs. If you've preserved and reviewed your bill stubs, you'll be aware of the new rates and able to cut back in discretionary areas to accommodate the jump in utilities expenses. If you're oblivious to the situation, you're likely to come up short each month and perhaps have to tap your savings to make up the difference. That's not the road to long-term success.

Most utilities, lending institutions, insurers, cable television companies, and other service providers will notify you of rate changes. Some will insert a separate notice in your bill; others may offer no more notification than a sentence on your statement. Pay attention to all these notifications and preserve them in your file cabinet. Here are other areas where comprehensive record keeping can help you stick to your budget:

Mortgage costs

Your home is your largest purchase; as such, the slightest change in your mortgage payments can knock your budget out of whack. Such changes are especially likely to occur when your real estate taxes and homeowners' insurance payments are rolled into your mortgage, a fairly common structure.

If a local taxing body increases its real estate tax rate, you'll need to calculate the effect on your budget and develop a plan to make up the difference. Many financial institutions analyze and recalculate mortgages only once a year. If that's the case with your mortgage, you can get hit with an increase in your mortgage payment going forward and a bill for past under-payment. If you don't stay on top of these issues, they can wreak havoc with your budget.

On the positive side, should interest rates decline, you may be able to refinance your mortgage and realize signifi-cant savings each month. You also may consider a home eq-uity loan as a less expensive option to such financing as a traditional automobile loan. This can be a double bonus, as interest on home equity loans often can be an income tax de-duction, depending on the amount involved and other factors.

You *can* take advantage of these opportunities—provided you're aware of your interest rate, mortgage balance and value of your home. Good record-keeping will help keep you aware.

Insurance

Know your deductible amount for every policy, and make sure you're aware of the potential savings that a higher deductible could bring. The savings each month could more than make up for the reduced payment you would receive in the event of a claim.

Employer-provided benefits

If you're like us, you received a thick packet of benefits docu-ments when you were hired, and you were so intimidated by its bulk that you put it aside for later reading. Time's up. Later is now. Break out that packet and review the documents, paying particular attention to any life insurance and disability insurance features.

These are great vehicles for you; if you had to purchase these policies yourselves, you typically would pay more than your employer is charging you. But is the coverage sufficient for your needs? Would it make sense to enhance your position with coverage that you purchase? If you leave your current job, would you replace your employer-provided coverage with policies you purchase, and what impact would that have on your budget? These are questions you can answer if you're familiar with your current coverage and costs.

Retirement plans

We've suggested before that maximizing your contributions to 401(k) accounts and other retirement plans usually is a great idea. But what happens if features of your retirement plans change? Clearly, you need to keep up with the plans and any modifications to identify corresponding adjustments that should be made to your financial blueprint.

Income taxes

As we've seen, your income tax situation can have a significant impact on your cash flow and your ability to adhere to your budget. Your income tax file will help you keep a running total of income, deductions, and withholding. Review your file at least several times a year so you'll be able to project any obligation or refund. Both, of course, can affect your budget.

Your review should include investments, which may be generating income and capital gains taxes throughout the year. If you're aware of this situation, you'll be prepared for some tax planning, including taking capital losses to offset capital gains, prior to year's end, when the rush to beat the deadline could lead you to ill-considered actions.

Record-keeping and your investments

Preserving and reviewing your records will help you stay on budget; it also will allow you to monitor your investments and adjust them as necessary. Here are the elements you'll want to document and track:

Performance

Establishing goals and the game plan to meet them inevitably involves many assumptions; investment performance is one of them. Your filing system should enable you to track the performance of your investments. Save all the reports so that you can compare the growth of your assets to the goals you've established.

You'll find that many investments perform inconsistently. A growth mutual fund may be up 20 percent one year, down 15 percent the next. That doesn't mean you dump the fund necessarily, but you do want to make sure the performance over time works for you and meets your assumptions. When taking an asset-allocation approach to investing, the overall performance of your portfolio is what's most important.

There may be occasions when you want to make changes. As you review the performance of your investments, compare it to the activity of other stocks, bonds, and funds within the same category or industry group and with the same management style. Again, the purpose of tracking these numbers is not to micromanage your portfolio by overreacting to daily surges or declines but to develop a method for tracking long-term performance.

Cost basis

Your records should include the cost basis for each investment. If you're contemplating selling an investment, you can check its cost basis to calculate the tax implications for your prospective gain or loss. This, of course, can affect your budgeting as well.

Balance

Your original asset allocation may provide excellent balance: a mix of industries, a blend of stocks and bonds, a dash of high-growth stocks, a dollop of blue chippers. That balance, however, will change over time as investments appreciate or decline. For example, you may determine that 25 percent of your overall portfolio belongs in international investments. If that group does well, it could become, say, 35 percent of your portfolio in short order. Now your position in international investments is proportionally greater than you intended, increasing your risk factor should that sector plummet.

To prevent this, you must periodically rebalance your portfolio to restore your original asset-allocation formula. If you preserve and monitor all the records related to your investments, you'll know when and how to rebalance.

Comprehensive record-keeping is not an arduous task, yet it's one that frustrates many otherwise conscientious couples. If pencil-and-paper tracking isn't your thing, you can do it via computer and the many software packages that are available for financial record-keeping. There's an added advantage with computer-based tracking: Many financial institutions offer on-line banking, with all transactions downloaded directly into your software package.

The services of a financial professional also can be helpful here, especially in tracking your investments and comparing their performance with that of other vehicles.

Whichever method you choose, the most important outcome is that both of you know where the documents are and have ready access to all of them. Always ask yourself this question: If I weren't here, would my partner know where to find our financial paperwork and which financial professionals to contact? If the answer is no, you have some work to do.

Pillow talk

Everybody loves a scavenger hunt; this one has important implications for you. Each of you should take the following list and round up as many of the documents as you can. Some are easier than others. You won't have any trouble with driver's licenses or Social Security cards, but what about that homeowners' or renters' insurance policy?

Give yourself a week or so to find all the items. Whoever finds more is the winner. Perhaps the loser should be assigned the task of starting files for each document or document category. We'll leave the rewards system to you.

You both come up winners, of course. At hunt's end, you're well on your way to comprehensive financial record keeping.

- $ Driver's licenses (copies only to be filed).
- $ Vehicle registration cards (one per vehicle, copies only to be filed).
- $ Auto insurance cards (one per vehicle, copies only to be filed).
- $ Social Security cards (copies only to be filed).
- $ Marriage license.
- $ Insurance polices (all coverage).
- $ Insurance premium pay stubs.
- $ Appliance warranties.
- $ Appliance maintenance agreements.
- $ Pay stubs (most recent will do).
- $ Employee benefits plans.
- $ Investment statements (all investments, including retirement plans).
- $ Credit card purchase receipts.
- $ Checkbook ledgers and canceled checks.
- $ Contractor estimates and receipts (for home improvements).
- $ Utilities statements.
- $ Income tax returns (federal, state, local, all years).
- $ Names/phone numbers of professional advisors.

Chapter 11

The Kids Factor: Financing Your Family Without Going Broke

Kids change the equation, don't they? With all the joy they bring, they still manage to turn your lives topsy-turvy—and your financial planning is no exception. First, there's the matter of who will stay home with the kids during their early years. No matter how you decide that one, as a couple it means fewer hours available for work and a corresponding decline in your income.

Then there are the immediate financial demands of raising children, which can be significant as well as unpredictable. Finally, there are long-term needs, such as college education.

Yet there are many actions you can take to finance your family without busting your budget. As in all matters financial, timely planning and joint discussions are the keys. Even if you're not starting your family immediately, the time to begin your planning is now. Your financial well-being depends in part on factoring family considerations into your current financial decisions. The impact will be with you for many years.

Before the kids come

As we've noted before, your home and your cars likely will be your largest purchases. If there are kids in your future, you'll want to consider the expenses of child rearing even as you determine which home and automobiles are right for you. This is especially true if one of you expects to leave a job and stay home with the kids. That will reduce your income appreciably, and it may be a signal that some trade-offs are in order.

Knowing that you'll have less income and more expenses when the kids arrive, it might be a good idea to purchase the smaller home and not commit to a mortgage that could prove back-breaking.

Other factors can influence your home purchase. If you're planning to send your kids to public school, are you happy with the school district in which your prospective home is located? Is the home you've targeted close enough to your place of employment to allow you to incorporate daycare, babysitter, and school pick-up and drop-off schedules into your routine? These are not, strictly speaking, financial matters, but they can turn into money woes quickly if you're forced to move because you find the school system inadequate or your commute too long to allow you to handle routine family matters.

Consider also the luxury of two cars. Can you get by with one car for now, filling in with public or pooled transportation? Be wary of creating a lifestyle that will prevent you from accomplishing the things that are really important to you, such as satisfying your children's needs.

Kid costs

Raising a family brings additional expenses, yet some will be offset, intentionally or otherwise. For example, you'll be spending so much time with your kids that you may not travel as much or dine out as often. You'll need to modify your budget to incorporate new expenses, insofar as these are predictable, and any savings. Some important new budget categories are:

Monthly essentials: formula, food, diapers, doctors, medicine

These expenses normally peak during your children's first few years—thank goodness. If you know which of these costs your health insurance will cover, you'll be better able to budget effectively. If you're not sure, retrieve that policy from your file cabinet and review it.

Childcare

Childcare costs can vary greatly, depending on family circumstances. If you need childcare, the costs can be substantial, even the pivotal factor in determining if one of you quits work to be home with the children. If you're working mainly to cover childcare expenses, you may well decide that it makes more sense to stay home.

Clothing

As long as your kids are living with you, they'll have clothing needs that don't diminish over time. They're always growing out of something or growing into the habit of demanding every article of clothing, down to the tiniest nose ring sported by their peers.

Think about several money-saving tactics here. One is hand-me-downs from family and friends. This can work well because kids usually don't wear out clothes; they grow out of them. So hand-me-downs can be perfectly serviceable. Also, when you're considering that home purchase, determine if the school district requires that students wear uniforms. This may seem a small item, but over time, it can bring tremendous savings.

Kids and your long-term goals

Inevitably, the costs of raising a family will disrupt your budgeting and financial planning. As new or prospective parents, part of your job is to keep those processes on track and maintain sight of your long-term goals.

When their children are born, many couples find they can't cover the new categories of expenses from income, so they raid the money they had earmarked for savings. They rationalize this by assuring themselves that it's only temporary. Once the kids are school aged, that money will be freed up for savings again, and they'll throw in a little more to make up for those few lost years of savings.

If only it worked that way. Instead of decreasing, today's parenting costs are replaced by different parenting expenses tomorrow. Lose the expense of diapers and you gain the cost of school clothes and supplies. Survive the burden of frequent doctor's visits and you encounter the bills for music or dance lessons. Something else always comes up; if you don't plan for that "something" and continue to rob your savings, you'll imperil your ability to achieve your long-term goals.

The best practice here: Assume that the cost of financing your family will increase, not decrease, over time. In fact, you can reduce it to a simple formula by figuring that your monthly child-rearing costs will increase at the rate of inflation, just as your other cost categories do. If you find you can't cover these additional costs through increases in your income, such as annual salary raises and promotions, then you need to sharpen your pencil and modify your budget—without dipping into savings.

Nothing can derail your journey to long-term financial security as surely and as swiftly as inadequate planning for the costs of child-rearing. Without proper planning, you find yourself using credit cards and increasing debt for the unforeseen expenses. You buy a second car—more debt—to enable you to chauffeur the kids around. But the biggest budget-buster of all is college education for your children.

The cost of college education has been soaring at almost twice the rate of inflation. From 1997 to 2001, tuition increases averaged 6 percent per year. If the spiral continues at this rate, the current annual average college cost of $13,000 will be more than $37,000 when your newborn goes off to Break The Bank U 18 years from now. If you don't begin saving for that now, or you shift assets targeted for savings to pay for current expenses, you could be forced to push your desired retirement date well into the future.

On the other hand, consider what happens if you're able to put money aside now, even in the face of your new family costs. Based on our previous example, today's $52,000 college education ($13,000 for each of four years) will cost $162,326 in 18 years, assuming an average 6-percent inflation rate. If you invest now, and if you can earn an annual rate of return of 10 percent, you'll need to save approximately $268 per month over the 18 years to realize the full college nut of $162,326.

However, if you don't begin to save until your child is 6 years old, when you imagine that you'll be past the heaviest kid costs, you'll need to save approximately $581 per month to achieve the same financial outcome. What a huge difference those six years make! The moral here: The earlier you save and the more you save, the better you'll be able to finance college education without sacrificing your other long-term goals, thanks to the power of compounding.

Few couples will be able to finance their children's college education from employment income alone. Therefore, it's important to begin planning for these expenses as soon as possible. Begin discussing this aspect of your financial game plan now. Do you intend to finance the entire cost of college yourselves? If so, how, and how much, will you save? If not, are you comfortable with student loans for your children that will send them into debt but help ease some of the financial burden on you? These are the questions to ask now.

Long-term financial considerations may even affect the timing of starting a family, to the extent that those things can be controlled. We know couples who have deferred starting a family for a few years to allow them to build up enough savings to accommodate the expected costs. Only you can determine if that's the wisest approach for you. But one way or another, the addition of children is an adjustment; you don't want to be worrying simultaneously about how you'll provide for them.

Your kids and your taxes

We hope that we've persuaded you of the importance of family planning, or at least of the financial aspects of family planning. (We'll leave the biological aspects to you.) If you're ready to plan, you're ready to consider such issues as how children may affect your taxes, how you can best address *their* taxes, and what vehicles are available to help you with the costs of college education. Fortunately, the government is aware of the exploding costs of child-rearing and has built some benefits and credits into the tax code. If you understand all the options, you'll be able to take maximum advantage of these benefits while maintaining a handle on your income tax situation.

Exemptions in swaddling clothes

Immediately following the birth of your child, you'll be able to claim the bambino as a dependent, picking up an additional personal exemption. You'll realize the full year's benefit no matter when during the year the child is born, even if it's on Dec. 31 at 11:59 p.m.

The IRS also provides a Child Tax Credit up to $500 per child. Under The Economic Growth and Tax Relief Reconciliation Act of 2001, this tax credit will increase to $600 in 2002 and then grow incrementally to a maximum of $1,000 per child in the year 2010. As we suggested in our earlier discussion of income taxes, deductions often come with a catch, and this one is no exception. The Child Tax Credit is phased out as you achieve certain income levels.

Childcare Credit

The government bases its Childcare Credit on a percentage of the costs you incur, as well your adjusted gross income. The more money you make, the less you're able to claim as a credit. To qualify for the credit, you'll need to submit information about your childcare provider (name, address, and tax identification number) to the IRS. Clearly, you'll want to determine up front if your prospective provider is a tax-paying vendor that conforms with any and all licensing requirements.

The good news here is that the Childcare Credit never entirely phases out. Also, be sure to check the status of your preschool and kindergarten, because costs associated with those activities may qualify you for the Childcare Credit. Keep that opportunity in mind as you evaluate preschool programs.

Higher education incentives

The government believes in higher education, so much so that it offers two education tax incentives. The Hope Credit provides families with tax credits up to $1,500 per student, which represents 100 percent of the first $1,000 and 50 percent of the next $1,000 spent on higher education. These amounts will be indexed for inflation beginning in 2002. The Hope Credit can be taken only during the first two years of undergraduate education, and it is phased out above certain income levels.

The Lifetime Learning Credit provides tax credits up to $1,000 per family; the calculation is based on a credit of 20 percent for up to $5,000 in expenses. In 2003, the maximum credit will increase to $2,000. As the Hope Credit, the Lifetime Learning Credit is subject to adjusted gross income phase-outs.

If you're eligible for both credits, you can select only one in a given year, although you're not locked into that choice for subsequent tax years. Do the math, and you'll know which is the better credit for you. As with all tax credits, eligibility requirements and income limitations can change, so keep as current as you can on modifications to the tax code.

The "Kiddie Tax" and related issues

Assets in your child's name can be a great savings vehicle for college education, but there are tax consequences that you must understand to view the entire picture of your tax situation.

In 1986, after noting with alarm the number of parents who were, in effect, shielding a portion of their income by stashing it in their children's names, the government imposed what has come to be known as the "Kiddie Tax." Under this provision, taxation on children's income is as follows:

Under age 14

$ Earned income up to the standard deduction is not taxed; earned income greater than the standard deduction is taxed at the child's rate.

$ Unearned income up to $750 is not taxed; unearned income from $751 to $1,500 is taxed at the child's tax rate; unearned income greater than $1,500 is taxed at the parents' rate, unless the child's rate is higher.

Ages 14 and over

$ Earned income is treated the same as it is for children under age 14.

$ Unearned income up to $750 is not taxed; unearned income greater than $751 is taxed at the child's rate.

Even beyond the tax consequences, placing assets in the names of your children raises questions of control. Who owns the investment? For what purposes can these assets be used? Can your children access the accounts? These can be troubling questions, without clear-cut answers. For example, if you place assets in your children's names, you may be less tempted to tap them, but what if you really need the money? Would you be comfortable using the kids' funds? Technically, it's their money and not available to you. On the other hand, if you keep the assets in your name, you may be more likely to draw them down for today's expenses, even though you conceived these vehicles as savings for college.

If you examine your current needs, long-term savings plan, and tax implications of any projected actions, you may arrive at the best answer for you. Keep in mind that when colleges evaluate applications for financial aid, they consider assets in the name of the child to be more "available" for college expenses than if they were titled to a parent.

Popular savings vehicles

The federal government, state governments, and some colleges themselves have established vehicles that will help you save for your children's education. Here's a look at some of the most widely used tools:

Custodian accounts

These accounts are based on the Uniform Gifts to Minors Act (UGMA) or the Uniform Transfer to Minors Act (UTMA); which is available to you depends on the state in which you reside. Generally, UGMA accounts are established in your child's name. As parents, you may contribute gifts of money and securities, within the rules for annual gifting, with taxes levied according to Kiddie Tax rules. At the age of maturity, all money in the account becomes your child's and is not restricted to educational purposes.

UTMA accounts are similar to UGMA accounts, but they typically are more flexible in the variety of assets they may hold, and they offer parents control of the accounts for a longer period than do UGMA accounts. Colleges consider each type of account to belong to your child when considering financial aid.

No matter which account you're using, all gifts are considered irrevocable and must be used to benefit the child. Make sure you discuss the tax and control issues before determining that custodian accounts are suitable for your family.

Education IRAs

Education IRAs allow for tax-free accumulation of dollars on behalf of a specified child, for qualified education expenses. They're a great way to save for education and maintain some control over the distribution of funds. Here's how they work.

If you establish an Education IRA, you may make annual contributions up to $500 per child under age 18—the ceiling increases to $2,000 per child in 2002—subject to income phaseouts. (Contributions are made with after-tax dollars, so there's no immediate tax savings.) The money also can be rolled over to another family member under 30 years of age, a feature that provides a measure of flexibility should the original beneficiary elect not to seek further education. If a balance remains in an Education IRA after the beneficiary reaches age 30, it must be distributed within 30 days, and the accumulated earnings become taxable.

Prepaid tuition plans

Many states offer prepaid tuition plans that allow you to purchase tuition credits with today's dollars to be used when your child reaches college age. The advantage here is that you avoid the impact of inflation on tuition, which has resembled a death spiral in recent years. Generally, these plans allow you to use your tuition credits at all schools within specified categories(for example, all state-related schools or all community colleges). In addition, a number of colleges and universities have implemented their own prepaid tuition plans, quite apart from state programs.

Such plans can bring you peace of mind, but be sure to examine all features. Can your tuition credits be used at colleges in other states? If your child elects not to attend college, is any or all of your money refundable? Even beyond these questions, you may feel strongly that what you invest on your own will outperform any prepaid tuition plan, that is, that the total of your principal and earnings from investments will exceed what tuition will cost 18 years down the road. In that case, prepaid tuition plans might not be the ticket for you. Few of us, however, are quite that confident about our investing prowess.

Section 529 savings plans

Authorized under Section 529 of the federal tax code, these are state-sponsored savings plans that offer a choice of investment options and allow you to name and change your beneficiary. You can invest in the plan of any state that offers one—you're not limited to your state of residence—and still use the proceeds at most U.S. institutions of higher learning. Some foreign institutions also may qualify. You'll want to research the various state plans to determine which has the investment philosophy and manager that best matches your needs.

Section 529 plans offer many attractive features. First, there's no phase-out ceiling, so high earnings don't exclude you. In addition, the contributions limit is quite generous. You can contribute to your 529 plan until the total account value—contributions and earnings—reaches $246,000. Next, your contributions receive special treatment for the purposes of gift taxes and estate taxes. Ordinarily, any gift you make in one tax year that exceeds $10,000 is subject to gift taxes. Section 529 plans permit contributions up to $50,000 ($100,000 for married couples) in any tax year without triggering the gift tax, as long as no further contributions are made over the next five years. Finally, distributions for qualified education expenses are tax-free.

These plans have been strengthened significantly in recent years. Prior to 2002, for example, the accounts grew tax-deferred, with distributions taxed at the child's rate. Now, there are no taxes at all on qualified distributions. Features such as these have made 529 plans the college savings vehicle of choice for many families.

When the day finally comes

Much of our preceding discussion has concerned ways to save for your children's college education when your kids are quite young. But when they're approaching college age, you can stay proactive by considering several types of assistance.

Financial aid

Most colleges and universities offer grants and loans that may be available to you. Usually, this assistance is based upon family need, although there are some aid packages awarded solely on the basis of family creditworthiness. Understanding the award process will help you with your financial planning. Here's some insight into the process for need-based awards.

The institution will ask you to provide your financial statements, including any assets in your child's name and any earnings your child may have. Based on your income and assets, the college will determine how much the family is expected to contribute to the child's education. They'll deduct that presumed contribution from the college's costs, and the difference is what they'll offer in aid. (Not all colleges will offer 100 percent of the difference on each occasion.)

You'll notice that a key factor is omitted from this calculation: your actual family expenses. Your income may qualify you for a certain level of aid, but if you're burdened with discretionary debt, you may not be able to make the contribution to your child's education that the college deems appropriate for your income. It's another reason to avoid discretionary debt.

When you and your kids are researching colleges, pay close attention to their financial aid practices and limits. In some cases, even the maximum aid package won't cover the costs at your child's first choice of institutions.

Scholarships

Scholarship awards, of course, depend primarily on the academic performance of your children. But you can help. There are an extraordinary number of scholarship opportunities available to students. If you take some time to surf the Internet, you'll familiarize yourself with scholarship opportunities you never dreamed existed. You don't want to count on these; proactive planning is by far your best bet for saving for college. But if your search does yield a scholarship opportunity, you're that much better off.

 *Pillow talk*

Everybody knows that kids can wreak havoc on the family budget. Just how much additional money will you need to generate for child-rearing? Here's a two-part exercise that will let you know what you'll need and how your budget must be modified to accommodate your new needs.

Part 1

Estimate the monthly costs for these child-related budget items:

New Budget Items	Estimated Monthly Costs
Formula	$_____
Food	$_____
Diapers	$_____
Pediatricians	$_____
Medicine	$_____
Childcare	$_____
Clothing	$_____
Total New Monthly Costs	$_____

Part 2

Now that you have an estimated total for child-rearing costs, get out your current budget and determine how you can meet these new needs. Ideally, a combination of new income sources and reduced expenses for discretionary items will do the job. However you approach it, don't touch the "Savings" category. You'll continue to need that money for your long-term goals, including college education for the kids.

Chapter 12

Estate Planning: Thinking About the Unthinkable

When you're single, you don't give much thought to the disposition of your assets and belongings that will take place after your demise or to the costs associated with the transfer of these items. Typically, you have no dependents, and you're not worried about providing for anyone when you're gone. Marriage changes your perspective on many things, including how you view the prospect and consequences of your own passing. You have a new priority: the financial security of your partner in the event of your death.

Part of your responsibility in financial planning is to ask the question: What if one of us dies? It's an unsettling question to be sure, but things can be a lot more unpleasant for the surviving spouse if you don't plan for this as a couple. In our insurance chapter, we discussed how to provide financial protection against the untimely death of one of you. In this chapter, we'll consider postmortem distribution of your assets and how you can assure they'll get to the right people with as little aggravation and delay as possible.

Contemporary estate planning has become more interesting and more complicated, in part because people are marrying later. In the modern marriage, both partners have been in the workforce for a number of years, and they've established passions and allegiances that they may want to address in estate planning. For example, if you've been involved with a charitable or nonprofit organization, you may want to bequeath some of your estate to that entity. Clearly, that's a discussion you'll want to have now with your spouse, because money left to a nonprofit organization is money that won't go to a family member.

In addition, the transfer of assets extends beyond investment accounts. You must consider your personal assets as well. Now that you're married, is your spouse aware of your intentions for your personal belongings? If you're the keeper of cherished family heirlooms, have you discussed how these will be passed on in the event of your death? If you haven't, you're just asking for family turmoil.

We know a pair of brothers who hold joint possession of a treasured asset: their baseball-card collection, which over the years has grown in value to thousands of dollars. They haven't discussed the disposition themselves, much less with their respective spouses and children, so they've never clarified what will happen to their ownership interests upon their deaths. The best guess is that a court will end up assigning a value to those Pete Rose rookie cards.

Your estate planning also must incorporate your dependents, whether children from a previous relationship or parents for whom either of you is providing care. You need to be assured that your dependents will continue to receive appropriate care. With proper estate planning, you can be confident that your assets will continue to meet the needs of your loved ones. And you can establish controls for your assets through the use of trusts, which is especially important if minor children are involved.

Finally, in planning for the disposition of your estate, you must consider the tax consequences. This is a priority. Estate taxes can chew up a bequest; it's not at all uncommon for heirs to be forced to liquidate assets they've inherited because they have no other way to raise money for the taxes. Federal estate taxes are the major concern, but income taxes and state inheritance taxes play a role as well.

Some couples unwisely put their estate planning on hold, misled by the prospect of relief from the Economic Growth and Tax Reconciliation Act of 2001. Although it's true that this act phases out federal estate taxes between the years 2001 and 2010, it's also true that what will happen after 2010 is unclear. In fact, the law contains a "sunset" provision: If Congress takes no additional action, estate taxes in the year 2011 will be reestablished at their 2001 levels.

In light of this uncertainty, addressing your estate needs now is more critical than ever, unless you're planning on expiring before 2011, an action we don't recommend. Just as the "after-tax" rate of return is pivotal for your investments, your "after-tax" estate balance is what will be most important to your heirs, and your ability to accomplish your goals in passing on your assets.

Beginning the process

Along with all other areas of financial management, estate planning is a process. Your lives will continue to evolve, which means your estate planning needs and desires will change as well. As you gain dependents and assets, you'll want to update your estate plan. Many couples think that titling every asset in joint name will solve all their estate-planning problems. As we've seen, this is not always the case. There may be better, more efficient ways to title assets to avoid additional costs at death.

Begin your estate-planning discussions by compiling a list of your assets, along with the titling and beneficiary designations (where applicable) for each. Also, talk about which people and organizations you want to inherit your assets and by what methods. Cover all situations, including the possibility of your simultaneous deaths and the more common circumstance of one spouse predeceasing the other. In that case, you must develop a plan for the death of the first spouse, and then again for the passing of the surviving spouse.

These are difficult, emotional discussions that sometimes can be made less wrenching by the involvement of a professional advisor. Your advisor will be able to detail specific estate settlement costs and ways to minimize those costs and help you prepare the documents you'll need for a solid estate plan. Remember, also, that estate laws vary from state to state and that you will need to review your estate plan if you relocate to another state.

Let's look at some of the basic documents to consider in your estate planning.

Wills

A will is one of the most essential and useful tools in estate planning, helping you accomplish many of your goals. It assures the distribution of your assets to the heirs you select, which is probably your primary objective. It allows you to appoint a personal representative to handle your estate affairs. Ordinarily, this will be your spouse, but you also may want to name a successor to your spouse, in case of simultaneous death or incapacitation. If you have minor children as dependents, your will can be used to designate a custodian for their care. If you're bequeathing assets to minors, your will can name a trustee to supervise the money. The custodian for the minors' personal care and the trustee for financial matters need not necessarily be the same person. In fact, you may prefer to name two people to build in some checks and balances. You also may use your will to establish trusts, designating exactly how you want your money to be distributed and when—an effective means of controlling your assets after you've passed on.

If you die "intestate" (that is without a will) the courts will make all of the aforementioned decisions for you. Your assets will be distributed according to your state's intestacy laws. These laws determine the pecking order for distribution of your assets. Typically, your spouse and children will be first, then parents, then siblings, and so on down the line. In many cases, the lineup is not what you would have chosen had you been around to make the call. You can avoid this unfortunate situation by creating a will.

Keep in mind that certain assets won't pass through your will. Titling, for example, takes precedence over your will. Therefore, if an asset is titled jointly with rights of survivorship, that money automatically goes to the joint owner, regardless of what the will may stipulate. If assets have beneficiary designations or transfer on death designations, these, too, supersede the will. If you're aware of this now, it can prevent a lot of heartache later.

As a couple, begin drafting your will now. You may seek professional advice, such as that offered by an attorney. Or you can pick up a standard template; these are available at legal supplies stores and even some department stores and pharmacies, believe it or not. The standard forms offer one-size-fits-all language that fits no one's circumstances snugly, but at least they'll get you thinking about various categories and provisions.

Power of attorney

Power-of-attorney documents are only slightly less vital than wills to your estate planning. Who will act on your behalf in times of emergency, illness, accident, or incapacity? Power-of-attorney documents specify just that, providing some financial protection against the unexpected. If you and your spouse maintain individually titled assets, your spouse doesn't have automatic access to assets in your name. Absent of a power-of-attorney document, a court would appoint someone to act on your behalf. Although this might well be your spouse, the red tape involved can be numbing and a frustration to avoid.

As with your will, name a successor to administer your power of attorney when you fashion this document.

Advanced medical directive/living will

These documents are used to appoint someone to make decisions for your healthcare needs, such as whether life support should be offered to you. You not only designate a decision maker, but you also have the opportunity to spell out your intentions.

Though their capabilities are much the same, there are differences between living wills and advanced medical directives. Living wills enumerate your specific healthcare wishes. Advanced medical directives are a subcategory of advanced directives (healthcare power-of-attorney documents would be another subcategory) and not living wills as such.

No matter the nuances, many hospitals require such a document before they'll admit you; if you don't have one, they'll provide you with an off-the-shelf document to sign. This usually is boilerplate that may not fully address your needs. In addition, if you're sick enough for hospital admittance, you and your spouse may not be in the best shape for this tough decision.

Because religious beliefs can inform living wills, you may wish to consult your family's clergyman about the specific provisions of your document.

As with all estate-planning documents, make sure to name a successor as well as a primary decision-maker. If you don't have this type of document and the need arises, the courts will appoint a guardian for you, which is never a desirable situation.

Wills, power-of-attorney documents, and advanced medical directives/living wills are the pillars of estate planning. Upon them, you can build a structure that allows for distribution of your assets and medical care for you, all according to your wishes. But the specifics of your plan also will be influenced by the costs of death. The two most significant cost categories are probate and taxes.

Probate

Everyone hates the word *probate*. It evokes images of inheritances wrapped in miles of red tape, endless sessions in court with eccentric claim-jumpers, and dollars lost irretrievably in the protracted process. Most people have that perception of probate without really knowing what the process involves, unless they've endured it.

Quite simply, probate is the legal procedure for passing assets to heirs. Probate is overseen by the courts; when you file your will and appoint your personal representative, you do so with the presiding court. Perhaps the most important aspect of probate to understand is that procedures, and therefore costs, vary from state to state. Sometimes, these variations are dramatic. To factor probate costs into your estate planning, you must become familiar with the protocol in your state.

In some states, for example, probate costs are relatively mild; if you reside in one of those states, creating a complicated estate plan to avoid probate may generate more expenses than probate itself. In other states, where probate costs are steep, adopting probate-avoidance measures may be useful.

One such vehicle is known as a "living trust," which, much like a will, specifies the distribution of your assets upon your death. The difference is that your assets are retitled in the name of the trust while you're alive. At death, these assets avoid probate and are distributed according to the trust. You'll accomplish the goal of avoiding probate, but living trusts can be expensive propositions, considering the costs for document preparation, asset transfers, and maintenance, which includes preparing and filing annual tax returns. Be sure to compare these expenses with the cost of probate in your state to determine the suitability of these vehicles for you.

Attorney's fees are another probate cost, one that probably is unavoidable. Almost without exception, you'll need an attorney to work through the probate process. In addition, the process usually requires the filing of an inventory of assets, estate tax returns, and inheritance tax returns. For these functions, you also may need the services of an accountant or financial professional, although it's not uncommon for estate attorneys to engage these consultants for you.

Some attorneys charge by the hour; others base their fees on a percentage of the estate. As a couple, you should take the time now to identify the arrangement you prefer and the estate attorney you would like to engage. This is not a decision to be made when you're grieving the death of your spouse. If an attorney is helping you prepare your will and other estate documents and you're happy with the work, why not tap that lawyer to oversee the administration of your estate? It will help streamline the process.

Assets that pass outside the will, via beneficiary designations or titling, to cite two examples, are not considered "probate assets," so they're not overseen by the courts. Be aware, however, that your attorney may include these in the calculation of estate administration costs.

Taxes

Death and taxes are no less certain than ever, but just how much those taxes will be is a volatile matter. Inheritance taxes in recent years have been the subject of considerable debate and modification on Capitol Hill, so it's wise to keep current on changes to applicable laws or check in periodically with your tax or financial advisor. Here's the current lowdown on taxes.

Federal estate tax

This tax, paid by your heirs, is assessed on the value of your estate at death. All assets are included in the calculation of the federal estate tax, regardless of whether they transfer via your will, titling, or beneficiary designation.

The impact of federal estate taxes will change dramatically between now and the year 2010, thanks to recent actions of Congress. Prior to the passage of the Economic Growth and Tax Relief Reconciliation Act of 2001, assets greater than $675,000 were taxed beginning at 37 percent, with a maximum rate of 55 percent. This was so onerous—the tax bite equaled more than half the taxable estate—that many beneficiaries were forced to liquidate the assets just to meet the tax bill. When the assets were small businesses, that meant loss of jobs and establishments that may have been vital to their communities.

Under the new law, the federal estate tax will be phased out; the maximum tax rate drops to 50 percent in 2002, and the tax disappears completely in 2010. At the same time, the amount of assets exempt from tax has been increased to $1 million for the year 2002 and will grow to $3.5 million in 2009; in 2010, all inherited assets are free of the federal estate tax.

As mentioned earlier, though, there's a joker in this deck. Absent further legislation, the Tax Relief Act "sunsets" in 2010; its provisions would become null and void. What Congress may be disposed to do about this situation is anybody's guess. We'll discuss this unpredictable situation shortly and its implications for your estate planning.

Another important aspect of this tax is that spouses can transfer property to each other and receive a full marital deduction. In other words, no federal estate taxes are due on assets transferred between spouses. As attractive as this seems, there are potential adverse tax consequences. If all assets transfer to the surviving spouse and the value of the estate is more than the exemption amount, that could generate a huge federal estate tax bill upon the death of the surviving spouse (depending upon the status of federal estate taxes).

Therefore, it may make sense not to pass everything to your spouse upon death. As an alternative, think about creating trusts to help shelter some of these assets from estate taxes. With trusts, you can provide income to your spouse and be assured that your assets will pass to your beneficiaries upon your spouse's death, without the burden of the federal estate tax.

State inheritance taxes

Many states impose inheritance taxes that are all but inescapable. About the only way to avoid them is to give your money away while you're alive. A noble action on your part, but gifts more than $10,000 per year, per person, trigger federal gift taxes. Keep this limit in mind before gifting any money to avoid state inheritance taxes.

Income taxes

The inevitability of inheritance taxes is pretty well accepted, but most of us figure that dying absolves us of income taxes at last. Alas, the IRS can reach you beyond the grave. Growth in such assets as IRAs, 401(k) plans, and annuities (remember that this income often is tax-deferred while you're alive) becomes taxable upon your death. (Roth IRAs do grow tax-free.) Because participants generally are funding these types of plans throughout their working years, the tax bill upon death can be overwhelming.

Once again, the good news is that most of these plans offer relief to your spouse, who can maintain their tax-deferred status by rolling the assets over into the spouse's name, as long as the spouse is listed as primary beneficiary. Beneficiaries other than your spouse may not receive this benefit to its fullest extent. In addition, if you list your estate as beneficiary, all taxes are due immediately upon your death.

Remember: A good estate plan addresses the consequences of what happens when the second spouse dies. The government has made it easy for assets to transfer between spouses. It's a mixed blessing because it makes the consequences of the second spouse's death seem less urgent. For the ultimate heirs, the tax ramifications can become pretty urgent, pretty quickly.

5 steps to a solid estate plan in uncertain times

The repeal of federal estate taxes, which will occur in the year 2010, has provided the ultimate rationalization for procrastinators everywhere. Why invest time and money in estate planning when the biggest expense goes away in 2010? The answer is simple: In the year 2011, the federal estate tax reappears in all its glory, unless Congress takes some action during these intervening years. The fact of the matter is that nobody can predict what this tax will look like in 2011 and thereafter. That creates uncertainty, which may be even more frustrating than a burdensome tax. (At least with that, you know what you're dealing with.)

The best bet is that the rules will change in 2011 in ways yet unknown. You can't wait until then to implement estate planning; if you do, you may miss your best opportunities to maximize your estate and minimize taxes for your heirs. Here are five steps to an effective estate plan in these uncertain times:

Step 1—Understand the purposes of estate planning.

Efficient estate planning goes far beyond the federal estate-tax structure. Maintaining control is an important objective. Your estate plan can control the distribution of your assets and the timing of that distribution. Always be aware of the costs—state inheritance taxes, probate expenses, income taxes—beyond the federal estate tax.

Step 2—Title your assets appropriately.

One of the most useful tools in estate planning has been "bypass trusts," which require assets to be titled individually. Bypass trusts enable couples to take full advantage of the "unified credit" (the amount that can be passed to your spouse without federal estate taxes). The 2002 exemption limit of $1 million increases to $3.5 million by the year 2009 before being fully repealed in 2010.

This relaxation of the exemption limit makes individually titled assets a better estate-planning tool for you than ever before. To maximize this benefit, the value of assets in each spouse's name should be equal to the unified credit amount, assuming there are sufficient assets. It's in your interest to pay close attention to the annual increases in the exemption limit outlined in the Tax Relief Act of 2001.

As with the federal estate tax, the exemption limit will revert to its 2001 level of $675,000 without further action by Congress.

Step 3—Keep good cost basis records.

The Economic Growth and Tax Relief Reconciliation Act of 2001 offers many benefits to those who effectively plan for them, but the law has some adverse consequences as well. One of these is the eventual repeal of the "stepped-up" cost basis received when assets are inherited. Currently, when heirs receive property, the corresponding cost basis is equal to the market value of the asset on the decedent's date of death. Therefore, when the inherited asset is sold by the heir, capital-gains taxes are minimized. This is a tremendous benefit—especially if the asset had appreciated significantly. Alas, this benefit is going away in 2010 on assets greater than $1.3 million for nonspousal transfers and greater than $4.3 million for spousal transfers. Assets exceeding these limits will retain their original cost basis.

Knowing the cost basis for each asset and keeping the documentation accessible won't help your heirs avoid capital gains taxes, but it will help you and your heirs with estate planning. It will reduce the time and costs in settling your estate, even as it minimizes potential problems with the IRS.

Step 4—Begin a gifting program.

If you intend to bequeath your money eventually—and if you know someone who's succeeded in taking it with him, give us a holler—why not develop a plan now to give some of it away? Gifting programs remove assets from your name, thereby reducing the size of your taxable estate and decelerating the estate's growth. Your beneficiaries don't pay gift taxes as long as your gifts are no more than $10,000 per person, per year; the compounding effect of your gifts can be substantial.

Even though the federal estate tax is due for repeal in 2010, the long-term prospects for the estate tax are uncertain. The cost of not gifting during these intervening years can be enormous, to say nothing of the lost opportunity to reduce state inheritance taxes and probate costs by thinning your estate.

If you do consider a gifting program, don't conceive it as a hurried, short-term ploy to diminish your estate and better qualify for Medicaid support that can make a nursing home more affordable. Under Medicaid eligibility rules, any outright gifts you've made over the past three years, and gifts to trusts over the last five years, are considered part of your estate. Thanks to these look-back rules, "instant gifting" can serve to delay your receipt of Medicaid benefits. Instead, think of gifting as a long-term program that you begin now.

Step 5—Consider life insurance.

Life insurance is a tried-and-true estate-planning vehicle. No matter how tax laws may change, a death benefit and accumulated gains from a life insurance policy always can help defray estate settlement costs. Don't take a "wait-and-see" attitude on this. As you age, the cost of insurance increases, even as your insurability becomes more speculative. A single bad medical test result or discouraging diagnosis can ruin your chances of ever qualifying for life insurance. You can always cancel a policy; you can't always get one.

 *Pillow Talk*

Effective estate planning begins with comprehensive understanding of both appropriate laws and your assets. Let's work on those assets.

As a couple, make a list of all your assets. Include columns for the current value, the beneficiary (where appropriate), and title.

When you've completed your master list, add the value of the assets titled to each of you as individuals. Do the same for the assets you hold jointly. You'll have three totals here—the value of assets titled to you, the value of assets titled to your spouse, and the value of assets titled jointly.

With this information in hand, you'll be well positioned to determine if, upon the death of either of you, most of the estate would be tied up in probate, leaving the survivor with inadequate cash and generating hefty attorney's fees. If you find this is the case, it may be time to consider a different titling approach.

Profile

Amy and Rob Smith:
Managing the Trade-offs

When Amy and Rob Smith wed in 1994, Amy was working at a diabetes center; Rob was establishing what could have been a lengthy career as a financial planner. Things didn't stay that way for long.

Emily, 2, and Linsey, seven months, soon entered the picture, even as Mom and Dad were changing occupations. Rob now works for a promising software firm that provides Web-based applications to some of the nation's biggest companies. Amy has temporarily left the job market to care for the girls.

Change and trade-offs have marked their marriage as they've tried to balance immediate needs and long-term goals. They've met the challenges with mutual planning and a healthy sense of humor.

"We have a heap in the back. We call it 'The Game Plan Heap,'" Rob jokes. "It's about eight feet tall."

Communication

"We don't schedule communications," Rob says, "but we talk as needed.

We'll get together, focus a little bit on money, and straighten out any problems."

Checking accounts, credit cards, and budgeting

Amy and Rob maintain one checking account, one savings account, and two credit cards. All are jointly titled, but as a result of their experience and discussions, they've designated Amy as manager of household expenses.

"I rely on her discipline, and I have no problem with it," Rob says. "Without her discipline, I would be a monster."

For her part, Amy handles these responsibilities sensitively.

"I don't mind paying the bills," she says. "That's kind of where I get my break from the kids. We tried it the other way and it just didn't work. It's not that big a deal. When we have more money, I'm not as disciplined as when we don't. If we're strapped, I will say, 'Watch what you're spending because it's close.'"

Trade-offs

Two key decisions have been instrumental in this couple's financial planning. The first pivotal choice was that Amy would leave her job to care for the kids, a choice both Rob and Amy support.

"The loss of her income was a tough nut," Rob says, "about a 35 percent reduction in our income. It takes away a lot of discretionary money. At the same time, we're both very happy for her to spend time with the kids."

Adds Amy:"I don't feel cheated. I don't feel like I'm missing out. We know it's expensive to live here, yet we choose to stay here versus another part of the country. There are still many things that we can afford to do."

The second major decision was buying an expensive Boston-area home that ties up much of their income in mortgage payments.

"You spend a lot of money for a house in the greater Boston area," Rob says. "It's still an entry-level house, but the trade-off is for the area. You don't get nearly the house, but you get the numerous advantages associated with the region. We did the right thing in buying the house, but I wish it weren't such a big payment each month. Then we'd have more money to save, invest, and do other things."

Both choices were right for this couple. They understand the trade-offs and are willing to live with the consequences, such as the nice, new, safe car that Amy and the kids enjoy and the "old junker" that Rob drives for his two-minute commute to the office. But they've also learned that trade-offs aren't forever.

"I definitely want to go back to work," Amy says. "It would be rewarding to get into a sales position with commission and bonus. I've been thinking about a travel agent's license. I'd not only make money, but it also would help us travel and visit our kids when they're older and not living at home."

Call that a savvy bit of long-term planning.

Planning and goals

College education for Linsey and Emily and a comfortable retirement for themselves are important goals for Rob and Amy. They've been planning regularly for those goals, only to discover that their blueprints require frequent modification—and sometimes consignment to The Game Plan Heap.

"We would like to retire early," Rob says. "My experience as an investment advisor taught me that retirement can bring fun and peace of mind. Our plans looked more promising before the bursting of the dotcom bubble. Still, I would like to launch my own company as a means of wresting control of our financial destiny."

For now, at least, retirement has become a less concrete goal.

"We'll retire when we're comfortable," Amy says. "There's no set age when we have to retire."

Investing

With Rob's background in financial planning, this is one couple that has little need for a professional manager. Their investments include mutual funds and individual stocks, as well as a life insurance policy on Rob.

"Mutual funds give us diversification," Rob notes, "but stocks are more exciting. When managed correctly, stocks also offer the opportunity for more rapid appreciation."

Advice

- $ **Rob:** "Invest early, and be aggressive. Use mutual funds, and when you buy them, hold them for the long term."
- $ **Amy:** "Save whatever you can, even if it's just a little bit. A lot of young people think they have forever to start saving. Then they look back and wish they had started a long time ago. You have to realize you won't be young forever."

Chapter 13

Prenups and Postnups: Where Romance and Finance Meet

The conventional wisdom long has held that if a couple engaged to be married needs a prenuptial agreement, they shouldn't be engaged to be married. How tragic, this line of thought goes, to plan for the end of a marriage even before the wedding ceremony takes place. The very words *prenuptial agreement* conjure up a stereotyped couple: a filthy rich old man trying to protect his bullion from a diabolical young gold-digger.

This may be the conventional thinking, but it isn't very wise. It's puzzling and disappointing that prenups have such a bad rap, considering how effective they can be in promoting a healthier marriage and, if they're ever needed, saving everyone time, grief, and money. When we utter the words *I do*, we pledge that only death will part us from our beloved...and we mean it. No one weds with the intention of divorcing, yet somehow, according to *DIVORCE Magazine,* 50 percent of first marriages break up within 10 years. If you don't plan for the possibility of death or divorce, the state will do all your planning for you, and

state law is notoriously inhospitable to the unique issues and personalities of your marriage.

If you consider all the financial documents we've discussed thus far, prenuptial agreements are among the most simple. Implemented before marriage, they're contracts that detail the status and ownership of individual and common assets, debts and obligations, as well as actions to be taken in the event of death or divorce. Postnuptial agreements are the same, but they're implemented after marriage; if you're reading this book as newlyweds, this chapter still applies to you.

We tend to hear about prenups only in association with celebrity split-ups, but they've become more popular in all walks of life. This makes sense. We're marrying later in life, bringing more intricate financial and family situations to the party. Prenups should be viewed as a tool to ensure fairness—fairness to each of you, who have worked diligently to acquire the assets you've brought to the marriage, and fairness to children and extended family members as well. A prenup can ease the anxiety that grips all members of your family when divorce looms.

If we haven't yet persuaded you of the value of prenups, consider them this way: The process of developing a prenuptial agreement can be the foundation for all your financial planning. In creating a prenup, you openly express your aspirations and concerns, fashion a plan to achieve financial security, and strengthen the bonds with your spouse in the process. Many religions require premarital counseling to ensure that all issues are aired. The process of creating and implementing a prenup does much the same thing, without the outside counselor.

The process

Before seeking legal advice or delving into the technicalities of the agreement, it's best to discuss the issues as a couple.

Without a third party in the initial stages, each of you will feel free to express your desires and fears openly. The discussion could become emotional, even cathartic, as you celebrate your shared vision but also recount your financial mistakes. Take your time with this, and avoid premature judgments. Put everything on the table, and encourage your partner to do the same as you work through the following steps:

Step 1—Disclose everything.

Ultimately, either or both of you may petition a court of law to enforce your prenup. The court will scrutinize the agreement closely, paying special attention to whether both parties were truthful about their finances. If you weren't, so much the worse for you. Thus, from a pragmatic standpoint, and in the spirit of love and affection that you should bring to this exercise, disclose everything to your spouse or intended. Your disclosure should include:

$ **Income sources.** Don't forget potential windfalls; inheritances, stock options, and proceeds from the sale of a business would be several categories.

$ **Debts.** Include any loans that you have directly or as a cosigner.

$ **Assets.** List anything and everything of monetary—and sentimental—value.

$ **Legal issues.** Disclose any criminal convictions, arrests, pending lawsuits, and court-supervised agreements, including alimony and child-support arrangements. You also should discuss the future exposure you may have to being sued, particularly if you work in a profession where malpractice litigation is common.

$ **Future financial responsibilities.** Do you anticipate that you'll be providing for your parents at some point in the future? That's a potentially significant expense that you'll want your prenup to accommodate.

$ **Lifestyle plans.** Kids are the chief issue here. Discuss how you'll finance your children's education and pursuits, such as music lessons and other extracurricular activities. Will one of you be interrupting your career to stay home with the kids? Many prenups factor in those years of lost earnings in arriving at a fair income and asset allocation plan.

Step 2—Ask these questions... and let fairness shape your answers.

As you consider the unappetizing prospect of divorce, you'll need to confront some tough issues now. In answering the following questions, fairness should be your overarching principle:

$ Which assets are individual, and which are marital? You may jointly decide that any property brought to the marriage, including appreciation on assets, gifts, and inheritances, belongs solely to the partner who brought them. Or you may decide that all property is marital property and subject to division at divorce. Be as specific as you like, especially in categorizing items of sentimental value, such as jewelry and heirlooms.

$ Who is responsible for the debts each of you brought to the marriage, as well as debt acquired during the marriage?

$ Who is responsible for satisfying a judgment or settlement in any pending or future lawsuit?

$ Should assets and income be divided equally or according to some other formula? The answer here may involve a determination of how much each spouse is contributing to the increase in the value of marital assets. Remember, "value" isn't always measured in dollars. Staying home with the children and taking care of domestic issues doesn't earn you a paycheck, but it has tremendous value that now must be quantified. As part of this discussion, you may decide to waive your rights to alimony or to predetermine a fixed amount or percentage for alimony.

Step 3—Implement a solid agreement.

Divorce laws vary from state to state; for that reason alone, it's wise to involve an attorney in the structuring of your prenup, after you've discussed your wishes with your spouse. Using a lawyer also will help insulate the agreement from a court challenge, provided that the agreement is fair; unfair prenups always are easily challenged. In fact, although a single lawyer may help you draft the prenup, it's best that each spouse engage an attorney for an independent review of the document. That way, it will be clear to any court that each spouse fully understood the prenup before signing it.

Build some time into the process. You'll need that time to digest all the provisions of your prenup and to make sure you're comfortable with them. If the document is signed under duress or unreasonable time constraints, it may not withstand a challenge.

Step 4—Review your agreement periodically.

Your prenup is not written in stone. You may, for example, include a provision to terminate the agreement after so many years of marriage. Or you may decide jointly to increase or decrease support levels over time. As you build your life together, your views and financial picture will change; your prenup can change with your circumstances, provided that both of you agree to any modifications to the agreement.

Postnuptial agreements

As mentioned previously, postnuptial agreements address the same items as prenups, but they're developed and implemented after the marriage. How do you introduce the subject of a postnup without arousing suspicions about your motives? For many reasons, none having to do with the imagined imminent demise of your marriage, postnups make sense.

If you've been up close and personal with the messy divorces of your friends, you may decide that a postnup will keep you from going down the same path. And if by so doing you alleviate the fear of an unfair, ugly divorce, each of you may feel empowered to be more supportive and caring. The flip side also is true: If you're haunted by fears of a one-sided divorce and don't address these concerns through a postnup, your fears could drive your relationship right where you least want it to go. Divorce, in that case, becomes a self-fulfilling prophecy.

Career changes, new business ventures, financial needs for children and aging parents—all are circumstances that could make postnuptial agreements useful and timely. Even without such conditions, every couple should consider a postnup, if only to keep the state from dictating the allocation of your assets in the event of divorce.

 *Pillow talk*

We have no clever exercises here—just plain ol' conversation. Discussion is at the heart of any prenuptial or postnuptial agreement, and don't expect to sign, seal, and deliver an entire document in a single session. Once you have a draft, walk away from it for a few weeks. Then take it up again to be sure each of you is comfortable with all provisions.

Begin your discussions by sharing your information in these key categories:

$ Income sources.

$ Debts.

$ Assets.

$ Legal issues.

$ Future financial responsibilities.

$ Lifestyle plans.

As you continue your conversations, you may decide that a prenup or a postnup isn't right for you. But your time won't have been wasted. Each of you will come away with deeper insight into what motivates your partner, and you'll have many of the fundamentals of a financial plan right there before you.

Chapter 14

The Second Time Around:
Love (and Finances)
Still Can Be Beautiful

Second marriages—and thirds and fourths for that matter—are a growing phenomenon. According to *DIVORCE Magazine,* 43 percent of weddings in America are remarriages for at least one partner. One might think that these unions would be more stable than first marriages. After all, both parties know the drill and should be more ready than ever to commit to mutual love and respect, to say nothing of joint financial planning.

The statistics, however, belie this cheery notion. *DIVORCE* notes that 60 percent of all second marriages end in divorce. We're not in the counseling business, but we can guess at some of the reasons behind these failures. First, whatever else it may be, divorce is draining, emotionally and financially. It leaves its victims feeling less than whole, eager to jump into a new relationship because it feels good to be loved again, not because it's the right relationship for the long-term.

Beyond that, divorce may leave its victims unwilling or unable to make complete emotional or financial commitments. One partner may enter a second

marriage determined that all assets will be combined, thinking that will reinforce the union. The other spouse, fresh from a scarring experience that involved asset consolidation, may mightily resist any suggestion of asset combination.

If you're marrying for the second time, you and your partner should pay particular attention to your financial health. Communication is even more important for second marriages. Although you face many of the same challenges as first-time newlyweds, the details usually are more complicated.

Full disclosure

You're having a romantic dinner with your second spouse-to-be. The candles are lit and soft music is playing. You gaze longingly into your lover's eyes and whip out two copies of your complete financial statement—one for you, one for honeybunch.

We admit, full financial disclosure can be a mood-breaker, but it's essential for a strong second marriage. You're a little older now; good or bad, you have a financial history. Both parties must fully disclose that history to begin planning your financial life together. Here are some components of the disclosure process.

Assets

Reviewing the assets each partner brings to the second marriage will enable both to understand what resources are available. Make your intentions clear as well. Been saving in a money market account for a new car? Let your spouse know that up front, so the purchase—and corresponding asset dilution—comes as no surprise.

Real estate should be a key part of your review and planning. At this point in your lives, each of you may own property or homes. You'll need to decide where to live, which property (if any) will be sold, and how you'll reinvest the proceeds of any sale.

Many couples find combining assets more difficult the second time around, if only because each partner may harbor a fear of "getting burned" again. Therefore, reviewing assets and spending plans can be a critical step in helping establish a sense of equality for each spouse.

Debts

The devil's in the debt, and things will get especially hot if you don't fully disclose your debts at the dawn of your second marriage. List your debts, and share the list with your spouse. Then, as a couple, develop a game plan for getting rid of the debt. You may decide to tackle all debt jointly, or you may prefer that each partner be responsible for retiring the debt he or she brought to the marriage. It can work either way, provided each partner has fully disclosed all debts and each is comfortable with the plan of attack.

If one partner brings significant debt to the marriage, both spouses need to understand the risks of titling assets jointly. That can lead to a situation where one partner end ups with responsibility, however inadvertent, for debts he or she didn't incur. There's nothing inherently wrong with this, provided that both parties agree to the arrangement.

As you enter your second marriage, each of you has established a track record on credit-card use. Make sure your discussion of debt touches on the future use of debt, with special attention to credit cards.

Income and career plans

Divorce often brings a comprehensive reappraisal that can include dramatic career changes. If you're considering new career options, remember to discuss these with your spouse. Quitting your job to return to school may be a laudable career choice, but if your spouse isn't expecting to become the sole provider for the household, your decision may not contribute to a lengthy marriage. Discuss any potential variances in your income so that you can build these into your financial blueprint.

Expenses

By this time, you've established spending habits and expenses, both fixed and discretionary. Disclose these to your spouse, and listen as your spouse discloses the same to you. Once you understand the full range of your expenses, you'll be able to budget accordingly.

Remember that these personal expenses are important to each of you. Don't be judgmental. Pronouncements such as, "If you work out at home, we can save on your monthly health club expenses," will provoke immediate resentment and problems down the road. Mutual respect is the proper approach here. Your ability to budget effectively and save for your long-term goals will evolve from understanding your respective spending habits.

Divorce-related issues and children from a previous marriage

Inevitably, if you've been married before, there will be issues that will carry over to your new marriage. Chief among them may be financial and/or custody arrangements for children from that first marriage. (You're not alone here. *DIVORCE* reports that more than 1 million children each year experience their parents' divorce.) Many such issues are controlled by courts, so it's essential that you understand the impact of your state's family law statutes as you're preparing to remarry.

Your divorce agreement could have a substantial impact on your new marriage. If you're paying or receiving alimony, don't assume that always will be the case. Many divorce agreements stipulate that if the party receiving alimony remarries and receives financial support in that new marriage, alimony ceases. Also, if you're marrying someone who's currently responsible for alimony payments, consider what a downturn in financial circumstances might bring. If your spouse is out of work, are alimony payments still required? If you file joint tax returns with your new spouse, does that make you responsible as well for your partner's alimony payments? These concerns may not be immediate, but they can become primary issues quickly.

Divorce agreements can affect your current union in still other ways. If you're divorced, imagine a situation where, as part of the divorce settlement, courts have assigned debt to your ex-spouse. Now imagine that your ex defaults on that debt. You could try explaining the court order to the bank, but they're likely to point out—and none too politely—that you helped to incur the debt and you're responsible for it.

The courts will help you go after your ex-spouse to re-cover the money. In the meantime, someone needs to satisfy the debt. If you want your credit to remain in good standing, that someone will be you. In addition, be aware that if you have joint assets with your new spouse, a portion of those assets could be liable for settlement of the old debt.

In a kinder, gentler era, these issues would have seemed hypothetical at best, insulting at worst. Today, they're simply commonplace. Because they are, you must include the financial baggage from your previous marriage in your current discussions on disclosure and financial planning.

College education

If you or your spouse has children from a previous relationship, it's important to discuss your game plan for financing the kids' college education. This is a timely discussion for all newlyweds, of course, but it's complicated by any arrangements you may have made with your ex-spouse. Will your new relationship cause any problems with those earlier arrangements? Will your new financial circumstances affect your eligibility for financial aid from a college or university? Be sure to explore these issues.

Your divorce may appear to be final, but in the modern financial arena, there's no such thing. Changes in marital status, income, or even residency could send you or your ex-spouse back to court to file a "motion for modification" of existing agreements. Thus, it's imperative that you discuss all possibilities with your new spouse. Surprises in this area can cause irreversible breakdowns in a marriage.

Special estate planning issues

When couples marry young, they experience life together and handle their responsibilities together. Many things aren't quite as straightforward when marriage occurs later in life, and that includes estate planning. One or both of you may need to consider care for children, elderly parents, or both. Estate planning will allow you to strike a balance between fulfilling your existing responsibilities and being a full-fledged partner in your new marriage.

Your will can help you maintain that balance. On the one hand, you can use your will to provide for children from a previous marriage as well as your parents. On the other hand, you can create "testamentary trusts" within your will to provide for your spouse. Such trusts provide income for a certain number a years before the corpus (principle) is distributed to an ultimate beneficiary.

You could, for example, establish a trust that would provide income to your new spouse throughout the spouse's life, with the balance distributed to your children upon your spouse's death. For aging parents, the mechanism is reversed. The trust's income underwrites their healthcare needs; upon their deaths, the balance is distributed to your children and spouse if you so designate. The combinations and stipulations are endless.

The long-term healthcare needs of you and your partner also may be a driving force in how you structure your assets and plan your estate. If you or your new spouse should require extended medical care or nursing-home admission, you may be forced to commit assets you've brought to the marriage to pay for that care—an especially worrisome consequence if you need that money to provide for other family members. Make sure you understand the full complement of insurance protection and healthcare insurance each of you brings to your new marriage; if there are gaps, you'll identify them in your discussions.

Finally, be sure to review all estate-planning documents each of you may have in place, paying special attention to titling as well as beneficiary designations on all insurance policies and retirement plans. At the risk of being redundant, we'll remind you that asset titling and beneficiary designations supersede your will. You may craft a wonderful estate plan that would provide handsomely for your children and other loved ones upon your death, but if all your assets are jointly titled with your new spouse, your plan never will be executed.

Prenuptial agreements

Many couples don't want to hear about prenuptial agreements, considering them tantamount to an admission that romance isn't as important to them as finance and that their union isn't likely to endure. We consider this a major misinterpretation. Instead, think of prenups as a mutual understanding that the road to eternal bliss is cratered with tough financial issues; a prenuptial agreement is a vehicle that helps you avoid the craters.

We're big believers in prenups for first marriages and even stronger supporters of them for second marriages. Couples with marriage experience usually aren't as touchy on this subject; they realize better than most the hazards ahead, and they have a clearer perspective on all the issues they may face.

Your prenup can be as broad or as narrow as each of you would like it to be. Due to the high failure rate of second marriages, we recommend you finalize your understanding as a prenuptial agreement, rather than fashioning a postnuptial agreement after the marriage. (See Chapter 13 for an in-depth discussion of prenups and postnups.)

Pillow talk

If you're young newlyweds enjoying the delights of your first marriage, feel free to skip this section and, uh, do whatever it is you do before retiring for the evening. However, if you've recently wed for the second time or are contemplating the same, here's an exercise that will take you and your spouse or intended along the road to full disclosure.

Each of you should make a list of the assets, debts, expenses, and other obligations you bring to the marriage. Your categories should be:

- $ Assets. Include the type and current value, as well as title and beneficiary (where appropriate).
- $ Property. List any property you own wholly or in part.
- $ Debts. Specify the amount and type (credit card, mortgage, and so on).
- $ Expenses. Take a pass at listing your current monthly expenses. List only your individual expenses; you'll address common household costs as you work out your budget.
- $ Obligations. Include child support and alimony payments, as well as support for any other dependents.

When you're ready, exchange lists. Chances are this will be the first time you're able to view, in its entirety, the financial picture of your new spouse or intended. Now, you're ready for joint discussions and planning.

Chapter 15

Shacking Up:
There Are Financial Implications

The high incidence of divorce has made the concept of living together without the benefit of marriage seem more attractive than ever. Many couples approach shacking up—cohabitation, in more formal lexicon—as a way to "try each other on for size" and make sure there's a fit before going through the legal process of marriage.

Records on cohabitation may be unreliable, because it's an informal arrangement in many cases and not always documented. Nevertheless, it does appear to be a growing phenomenon. In March 2001, the U.S. Census Bureau reported more than 4.7 million American households of "two unrelated adults of the opposite sex," an increase of about 5.6 percent from the previous year. More than 35 percent of such households include children under 15, making financial issues particularly significant.

What's lacking in the statistics is any solid evidence supporting the notion that cohabitation before marriage makes for a more lasting union. Some couples discover the fit is less than perfect and never

make it to the altar. As a result, cohabitation can be emotionally and financially unsettling. If you're involved in such a situation or considering one, this chapter should help you protect your resources and provide some financial stability.

Cohabitation *does* have some financial benefits. Due to the higher tax rates for married couples relative to single individuals, the loss of eligibility for certain deductions, and the adverse impact on the prospect of financial aid from colleges, tying the knot can bring a limited number of financial disadvantages. But they're not so numerous or weighty that they should drive what could be the most importance decision of your life. Further, there are huge financial negatives that could prove ruinous.

Protection

If you live together without marriage, your focus should be asset protection for each of you. States don't offer you the same types of protection, such as equitable distribution and support, that they do for married couples. Some states still recognize common-law marriages, in which the partners are considered legally married if certain criteria are met. The most important standard usually is the length of time you live together, but the criteria also may include filing joint tax returns, adoption of your partner's name, and openly considering yourselves to be husband and wife. Requirements vary, so it's essential to know the law in the state where you reside. Common-law states are:

$ Alabama.

$ Colorado.

$ District of Columbia.

$ Georgia.

$ Idaho (if created before 1996).

$ Iowa.

$ Kansas.

$ Montana.

$ New Hampshire (for inheritance purposes only).

$ Ohio (if created before October 1991).

$ Oklahoma.

$ Pennsylvania.

$ Rhode Island.

$ South Carolina.

$ Texas.

$ Utah.

Palimony

Much like prenups and postnups, the popularity of "palimony" was fueled by the high-profile break-up of celebrity couples. It's like alimony in that one party voluntarily or under court order agrees to provide the other with financial support upon the dissolution of their relationship, but it's called palimony because the partners never wed. In principle, it sounds like a useful measure of protection. In the real world, palimony lawsuits can be difficult to win because you must prove that your partner made financial promises that were not kept. In addition, treatment of palimony lawsuits varies from state to state.

Because common-law designations and palimony verdicts are so speculative, it's unwise to count on them or to base financial decisions upon them. Here's a good rule of thumb: Don't make any changes in your life that you wouldn't be happy with if you were living on your own again. These include career changes, relocation, or selling your residence to move in with your partner. If any such change would make you more dependent on your partner, take a devil's-advocate approach and ask: If I make this change and things don't work out, will I regret it?

Debts and assets

No matter how deeply you feel for each other, it's a bad idea to take on any of your partner's debts. Further, avoid any purchases in joint name; if your partner doesn't pay his or her share, you will be fully responsible for that debt. Even if you have a written promise from your partner to pay, your creditor won't care. To protect your credit rating, you'll likely end up satisfying the debt and going to court to try to collect reimbursement from your partner. This is a nasty situation, one you can avoid with a little planning.

Some joint commitments, such as signing a lease together, may seem unavoidable. Understand that if you do this and your partner goes south, each of you remains responsible for the commitment. If you're the one who stays local, can you guess who your landlord will come after?

The prospect of purchasing a home or other property together raises the same sorts of troubling issues. Our opinion is that if you're not able to commit to each other via marriage, then you shouldn't be committing to major joint purchases, either. It can cause serious emotional and financial stress if the relationship terminates.

Be equally cautious with your assets. Don't give your partner access to your checking and savings accounts, investments, or personal property, such as cars. If you own assets jointly, each party typically has full rights to those assets. That means your partner could sell or liquidate assets or accounts without your knowledge or consent.

The right way to do it

Some people prefer shacking up to marriage because the less formal approach appears to preserve their options while maximizing spontaneity. At the risk of sounding like fuddy duddies, let us remind you that you won't have many options at all if an ill-planned cohabitation arrangement erodes your finances. There's a right way and a wrong way to approach cohabitation. Here's the right way.

Discuss and disclose everything

Throughout this book, we've stressed the primacy of regular and open communication as the foundation for financial security and the fulfillment that security brings. This is no less true because you're cohabiting rather than married. Just as you evaluate the compatibility of your relationship in a number of key areas—hobbies, sex, favorite vacation spots—so, too, must you consider your financial compatibility with your partner. That means full disclosure. If you think that shacking up empowers you to be less than forthcoming, you'll be dooming the relationship from the start.

Implement a cohabitation agreement

Similar to prenups and postnups, cohabitation agreements are implemented in the same fashion and treated with the same care. Cohabitation agreements are easier to discuss and accept than prenups and postnups because you and your partner understand that your relationship might not endure. Therefore, you're more receptive to the idea of an agreement that defines the financial aspects of your relationship. Then, if the relationship does blossom into marriage, you'll be one step ahead of the game; you can implement a prenup as a logical continuation of your cohabitation agreement.

The document should encompass assets, debts, personal belongings, financial obligations you anticipate undertaking individually and jointly, and support issues. As with prenups, each of you should have your own attorney review your draft agreement. Your attorneys also can advise you about the validity of cohabitation agreements in your state.

Develop a household spending plan

One of the advantages of living together is that you can share household expenses. But who will pay which bills? Remember, if your name is on a bill, you're responsible for it, no matter the whereabouts of your partner or his or her willingness to share the expense. This is a protection issue that you must consider.

Engage in estate planning

If you're enjoying a successful relationship and anticipate staying together, you'll want to consider the passing of your assets upon your death; married couples go through similar deliberations. If you want your estate to go to your partner, make sure that's reflected in the beneficiary designations on life insurance and other retirement plans. Your will also can be a useful tool in ensuring that your partner benefits from the distribution of your estate.

Because of the nature of cohabitation, we do advise that you avoid irrevocable actions in your estate plan.

 *Pillow talk*

If you skipped over the prenup and postnup planning exercise in Chapter 13 because you don't believe marriage is in your future, we're not letting you off that easy. Now is the time to undertake this process as a couple to begin formulation of your cohabitation agreement.

Discuss and fill in the following categories:

$ Income sources.
$ Debts.

$ Assets.

$ Legal issues.

$ Future financial responsibilities.

$ Lifestyle plans.

Once the numbers are penciled in, talk about how your assets will be merged or separated and who will be responsible for current debts as well as future expenses. That will provide you with the framework for your agreement.

Your attorneys should review the working document. And don't overreact to the draft, as these often are emotionally charged issues that provoke equally emotional responses. Come back to it in a week or two to better gauge your comfort level.

Profile

Shirley and Stan Angrist: Passing the Test... with Flying Colors

When Shirley and Stan Angrist were well into their 50s, Stan decided that he would take over their portfolio management from their financial advisor. After all, he had financial expertise and credentials (as a former reporter for *Forbes* and the *Wall Street Journal*) that few people can boast. He's so financially sophisticated that he and their sons Misha and Ezra a few years later would launch Biotech Horizons Fund, LP, a "hedge" fund that operates much as a mutual fund, except that investments are "hedged" with a mix of short and long positions as well as options. They continue to operate the fund today.

But joint planning has been a hallmark of this 46-year marriage, and when they sat down to mull over Stan's decision Shirley expressed more interest in their portfolio than ever before.

"I decided I really had to know more about all this," Shirley recalls. "I said to myself, 'You shouldn't be like all those other women, many of them

widows who don't know a thing about what's going on.' I began raising questions, asking Stan if we were getting as much from our investments as we should."

Shirley proposed a challenge. Stan could take over their portfolio, provided he outperformed their current manager in a two-year test. Though stunned initially, Stan ultimately warmed to the task. After a year, Stan's performance was so superior that he was declared the winner of The Shirley Challenge and handed the reigns of the family portfolio.

"I was relieved," Shirley says. "I thought that nobody could do better than Stan, but I needed to be sure."

That incident is representative of this Pittsburgh couple's joint approach to the challenges of marriage. Their careers have brought a number of dramatic changes. Both began as faculty at Carnegie Mellon University (then Carnegie Tech) Stan in engineering, Shirley in urban and public affairs. Stan left the university for journalism, deciding later in his career to freelance (he still writes book reviews for the *Journal*) and help operate the hedge fund.

For her part, Shirley worked in government affairs for PPG Industries and, though semiretired today, continues to serve some freelance accounts. Shirley and Stan even took a joint fling at entrepreneurship, founding and subsequently closing a remaindered book business and a make-it-yourself jewelry shop.

"We didn't sell enough books, and we didn't sell enough jewelry," is Stan's postmortem analysis of their retail ventures.

Their marriage has been filled with such tests, and they've passed them all with flying colors.

Asset consolidation

"When we got married," Stan says, "everything I owned fit into the back seat of a Buick. An old Buick. There weren't any assets to talk about."

Although it wasn't an issue early, over the years Shirley and Stan did devote time to proper titling of the assets they acquired throughout their marriage.

"We keep some assets in separate names," Shirley says. "That way, either of us can inherit assets in the other's name, but neither of us is stuck without our own assets. If probating the will takes time, you have your own kitty."

Budgeting

Ever the numbers man, Stan decided early in their marriage that he would record every household expenditure.

"I did it for maybe three weeks," he says. "Then I said, 'This is crazy. This is a pain. What do I know now that I didn't know before?'"

Today, Stan uses a popular software package for budgeting and accounting purposes. For longer-term matters, the couple relies on regular communication.

"We have a monthly review of our portfolio," Shirley says. "If we're doing well I congratulate Stan. If we're not, I ask why."

Checking accounts and credit cards

They have two joint checking accounts. Stan pays most of the bills; Shirley handles such items as charitable contributions and gifts, including gifts to three sons, Joshua, Misha, and Ezra, and their families.

Shortly after their marriage, Shirley and Stan discovered a philosophical difference about credit, stemming in part from Shirley's upbringing in her native Montreal.

"Because I'm originally Canadian, I have some pretty conservative ideas about money," Shirley says. "In Canada at that time, it was not common to buy on credit. So our first financial quarrel—call it an issue—was whether to buy a car and furniture on credit. I talked to some friends who also had come to this country from Canada, and they said there's nothing dangerous about credit. That was my first lesson in a different way of looking at finance, my first lesson in becoming an American."

They've continued to keep the danger out of credit-card purchasing.

"We have one credit card, and we're their worst nightmare," Stan says. "We pay in full each month."

Trade-offs

Purchasing their first home required virtually all of their $6,000 savings. Although it limited their ability to save in those early years, it proved to be a valuable investment. You don't get 37 years from most investments, but that's how long Shirley and Stan lived in that first home.

The decision to raise a family presented more difficult choices.

"We felt it would be more important for Stan to work full-time and for me to work part-time," Shirley says. "That was rough for me—part time, then full time, then part time again, but it worked out. I paid something of a price in my career for that, but when I look back on it, if we wanted to have a family as well as two careers, that was the way to do it."

Investments and long-term goals

Since winning The Shirley Challenge, Stan has spent about 20 hours each month managing the couple's portfolio. He also manages his mother's assets and, just for fun, runs several portfolio contests for a group of friends. The key to his money-management approach is diversification; a diverse portfolio reduces risk.

Stan regularly tracks a number of mutual funds, applying formulas to determine the correlation between any pair of funds. He won't buy into any fund that correlates strongly with any of the couple's current investments.

"That would give you a duplication of values," he says. "That's great if prices rise, but if they go down, you get a double hit."

Because of the great variety of their work experience, their retirement benefits are somewhat choppy. Shirley took a major step to a secure retirement for the couple by maximizing her 401(k) contribution at PPG.

Advice to newlyweds

$ **Stan:** "Couples should start investing—even in a small way—right after they get married. It will pay off in terms of achieving longer term goals, such as buying a house, sending kids to college, and retirement.

"Study market history. People are way too willing to listen to brokers and financial planners whose long-term interests are not necessarily parallel with those of their clients. If you can spend just an hour getting the ideas behind modern portfolio theory, over your lifetime it could save you hundreds of thousands of dollars."

$ **Shirley:** "How you manage your money, who has the right to do what, how much consulting you do with each other—all that needs to be laid out very early. If you make it an ego battle, it will hurt the marriage. It has to be win-win.

"I don't approve of the *laissez faire* approach, where the man manages everything and the woman sort of goes along and every now and then discovers how ignorant she is. Couples need to be open with each other and put their concerns on the table very early."

Index